MW01626199

ISBN 978-0-9788845-0-3

Printed in the United States of America.

Published by: BSRS Publishing, LLC

CHAPEL HILL, NC

U . S . A.

Ver 2.0

Pat,

Enjoy the book and the insights which can help!

Borrow Smart Repay Smart

REDUCE YOUR COST
OF HOME OWNERSHIP
BY $1M OR MORE

Todd K. Ballenger
Daniel Williams

Contents

Part I

Part II

The composition of this book has been for the author a long struggle of escape, and so must the reading of it be for most readers if the author's assault upon them is to be successful, — a struggle of escape from habitual modes of thought and expression...

The difficulty lies, not in the new ideas, but in escaping from the old ones...

John Maynard Keyes,
from his preface to The General Theory of Employment, Interest and Money, 1935

"Those who understand interest – earn it.
Those who don't – pay it" -- Albert Einstein

Part I

Foundations

A house is a place to live and work, but it is also an important part of your wealth creation. In this book, we'll develop your personal plan to minimize your cost of housing ownership. Whether you are buying now, refinancing now, or find yourself many years into an existing mortgage, you're certain to profit from this experience - whether you choose to borrow, or pay cash.

A house, or a home? A house is the physical shelter, the wood or brick, the shingles, the windows, and the doors. Your sense of home comes from the experience you have living in a house, but it is not the house itself. A house provides a place to raise a family, enjoy hobbies, socialize, sleep, relax, and more. We equate the personal experience of home with the physical house that makes that experience possible. The ability to separate house from home makes it easier to consider the impact the house has on your overall wealth. It costs real money to live inside, and how much money is a function of how well you understand interest.

When you invest your money in the stock market, you hold an asset that can go up or down in value. What about real estate? House prices, like stock prices, can go up and down. The most recent housing crisis of 2008 created a tipping point in our awareness about how the house needs to be managed to minimize risk, as a threat to the house will impact our experience of home. The house sits at the crossroads of our most important dreams, personal and financial goals and aspirations.

House equity—the net value of a house (minus) your current debt—is the most common form of wealth in the United States today. While your house may be your largest asset, your mortgage may be your greatest liability. Trying to manage your assets without learning to manage your liabilities can be like heating your house with the windows wide open.

Imagine - during your life you will borrow money you want but don't have, and lend (invest) money you have but don't need. Your entire financial life will act as a record of the decisions you made to borrow and lend money over your lifetime. Like interest, good or bad decisions typically compound over time.

This book will help you understand how the house fits into your overall financial portfolio, how interest work, how to borrow and how to repay your borrowing. You will learn that "location, location, location" is no longer just about the physical location of the house, but the location of your house equity as well.

In this book, you will discover how to manage your house:

- As a part of your personal wealth
- To support changing cash flow needs
- To minimize your cost of ownership
- To provide additional income during retirement

We'll discuss how the two different types of borrowers (the debtor and the creditor) use their house differently as a foundation for creating wealth. We'll explore the concept of being debt-free while still having a mortgage.

Humanist psychologist Abraham Maslow proposed that our needs are satisfied in a particular order: first we satisfy our physiological needs (food, water, shelter); then we focus on safety and security; next we begin to focus on family and community, followed by personal ego and self-esteem; and finally comes self-actualization.

The house helps us provide for our physiological needs, our safety and security needs, our family and social needs, and, to some extent, even our self-esteem (since house ownership reflects recognition and status). The house creates a foundation for personal growth, and it can be a primary foundation for your personal wealth development.

Part 1 of this book asks you to look at the house in the same way you look at your investments. What does it truly mean to manage liabilities?

Part 2 of this book offers a 7–Step Borrow Smart plan. This step-by-step approach will guide you through a simple decision-making process to identify a clear strategy for new borrowing. If you are in the middle of a purchase or refinance transaction now, it might be best if you read Part 2 -- the Borrow Smart 7-Steps to help with a current decision.

Whatever your destination, the collective insight in this book will help you reach your goals faster than you may have ever thought possible. ▪

Chapter 1

Wealth and the House

"Every person who invests in well-selected real estate in a growing section of a prosperous community adopts the surest and safest method of becoming independent, for real estate is the basis of wealth." -- Theodore Roosevelt

Real estate appreciation continues to reshape Americans' net worth. The Case/ Shiller index, reports that real estate values declined for almost 50 years from the late 1800's to the 1940's, then grew 40% over a 5 year period - marking the end of World War II. Property values then moved up and down slowly in a 15% range for another 50 years from the early 1950's through the late 1990's before increasing 90% in an astounding 8 year rally that peaked in 2006. Since then, values have declined 6 consecutive years, stabilizing in 2012 before shooting up again over 20% in the last few years. If the cycle holds, we are due for another 50 year period of values moving up and down in a 15% range.

While money travels electronically at the speed of light and fewer and fewer financial transactions involve physical money, we view the house as more tangible than a wire transfer, more beautiful than a dollar bill, and more resistant to change than a stock. If you've purchased a house in the last 10 years, you may have seen a volatile 35% move higher or lower in your house value.

For most Americans, the house has held its value over time, with much less volatility than other investments. For many, the leveraged growth of house appreciation has helped the house become their largest single asset. While we know it costs extra to live inside, and the house for most of us is traditionally a home first, a place we live our lives, we also know the house impacts our wealth. It could very well be a source of income in retirement.

Your House Wealth

How is house wealth determined for an individual owner? The wealth in a house is its current value minus any liabilities against the house.

Do you manage your house wealth as carefully as you manage your other investments? Give this question serious consideration. As demographic changes and interest rate fluctuations continue to impact the economy, and as life expectancy continues to increase, the house will play a growing role in your financial future.

Currently, just over 2/3rds of American adults own a house. Economic forecasters expect average house prices to grow, albeit at a slower pace and with less volatility than in recent years. As baby boomers age, older houses are torn down, new families form, and a growing numbers of immigrants buy houses, the real estate inventory must grow to keep up with demand.

The most basic purpose of a house is to provide a place to meet our physical needs for safety and shelter and our social needs of family and community. If it stopped there, most of us would live in a simple rectangular structure with a roof, or we would rent a house rather than committing to a long-term loan.

In a prior Fannie Mae National Housing Survey, Americans' top reasons for owning a house were: security, freedom, independence, privacy, and pride of ownership. In Fannie Mae's more recent National Housing Survey, consumers cited Long Term Financial Investment as one of their top reasons for buying a house.

We have come to assume that our basic physical and emotional needs are part of a package of value related to "the feeling of home ownership." In deciding whether to buy, sell, or hold a property, we now give a great deal more consideration to the logical investment aspect of the house and its impact on our wealth. Can we afford to sell now? Should we buy now or wait? Should we sell and buy something smaller, or larger? Should we refinance now and increase our monthly savings, or reduce our mortgage term?

Homeowners expecting to live in a house for a relatively short time face greater market risk from interest rate or valuation changes than those who stay longer. Renting often makes more sense if your time frame for ownership is 3 or fewer years.

The High Cost of Renting

In the 1990's, there was a great deal of discussion about the difference in lifetime earnings of a high school graduate versus a college graduate. The gap has closed somewhat, but it still remains. According to the last U.S. Census Bureau study, the average high school graduate will earn an average of $24,572 per year over the span of their career, while the average college graduate will earn $45,678 per year. That's a difference of more than $1 million during their working careers. Thus, one must look at the cost of college as an investment, not just an expense.

Could there be a similar comparison between renting versus owning a house? How much more wealth, on average, is created by buying a house? To understand this, we must better understand how owning a house creates wealth.

The House as a Wealth Creation Tool

Increasingly, the house is the key building block for wealth creation. Most consumers cite "buying a first house" as the reason they began saving for the first time, but many Americans believe that they needed to save 20% to buy that first house. Today, this is rarely true. If your savings growth fails to keep pace with rising house costs, you actually lose ground.

Buying with little or no down payment may be a better alternative if you think house prices will increase in value. Let's say you have $5,000 now, but want to save $20,000 total to buy a house worth $200,000. You can save $375 each month over and above your rent. It would take you about 3 years earning 2% net after tax in a savings account. Your balance after 3 years is $19,210. The house you wish to purchase appreciated at 2%* each year while you were saving. The house you wish to buy now costs $212,241. While you were saving the additional $14,210, the house increased in cost by $12,241. If you had purchased the house with the $5,000 you had 3 years earlier, it would be worth $212,241. You would benefit from the appreciation, the rent would have become principal reduction to reduce your mortgage balance, and the extra savings could be used to offset any additional mortgage insurance and be used to further reduce the mortgage balance. **It is likely the house will appreciate at a much higher rate.*

Cost of Saving to Buy a House					
Savings *2% Growth Rate**			Real Estate *2% Growth Rate*		
	Value	Change		Value	Change
Day 0	$5,000	n/a	Day 0	$200,000	
Year 1	$9,642	+$4,642	Year 1	$204,000	$4,000
Year 2	$14,378	+$4,736	Year 2	$208,080	$4,080
Year 3	$19,210	+$4,832	Year 3	$212,241	$4,161
Additional Savings		$14,210	Additional Cost		$12,241
**assumes after tax growth rate, annual compounding*					

We assume in this example that your rent would approximate any interest paid on a mortgage. If you misunderstand the high cost of waiting in an appreciating real estate market, you could miss your entry point and never catch up by trying to save more. Talk to a Realtor® and look at trends in housing prices in your local market. There are always going to be times when renting makes more sense than buying. For example, temporary housing may be necessary during a job transition or a divorce. Or, if house values in your area are decreasing, or highly inflated, it might be smart to rent for awhile.

Looking at the Long Term

The house offers shelter and a place for comfort, enjoyment, relaxation, and privacy. While there is nothing wrong with enjoying your house purely as a home and investing your savings elsewhere, it is worth exploring how the house compares with other investments over time. The house is a unique investment consideration, it's a cost and that cost can vary greatly over time. Minimizing that cost increases your ability to save.

For many Americans, more money will likely flow through their house than will ever flow through their other investments. Properly managed, your investment in the house could account for thousands, and even millions, of dollars in potential new wealth over your lifetime.

Consider a house that could be purchased for $200,000 cash. That house appreciates 3% annually. In 30 years, it would be worth $491,902. Consider that the same $200,000 could have been invested elsewhere at a 6% annual rate of return. In 30 years, it would be worth $1,209,748.

That's a difference of $717,846, over 3 times the amount you borrowed. The degree to which you learn to borrow smart and repay smart will determine the degree to which a portion of that $717,846 increases your wealth, as opposed to the wealth of others. The wealth will be created either way. Do you pay cash for your house, or borrow? Do you put extra cash flow toward repaying your mortgage, or into an investment account?

Imagine that you bought that house for $200,000, and in reading this book you realize you could refinance to a lower rate, change your loan product, change the way you repay your mortgage, or any one strategy saves you $261 per month (we'll talk about this more in the chapters ahead). If learning to Borrow Smart or Repay Smart saves you $261 per month, that savings invested at 6% over the life of the loan would grow to $262,907, more than what you paid for the house.

$261 Saved Monthly on $200,000 House Purchase		
Invested at an 6% Annual Growth Rate*		House Price
Month 1	$261	$200,000
Year 1	$3,219	
Year 10	$42,806	
Year 20	$120,800	
Year 30	$262,907	
*growth considered as after tax return		

If you begin to view the house as part of your investment portfolio—as another tool for long-term wealth accumulation or protection—you will bring your attention to that wealth. If you pay attention to your house investment, you are more likely to manage that equity (and the related liabilities) more effectively to increase cash flow. If you are willing to take that cash flow and save or repay in the most efficient way posisble, you'll find this one of the best returns you've made in your financial life. To do this, we need to look closely at how the house investment compares with other types of investments, based on common criteria for choosing among different investment products.

Summary of Key Learnings

- *It pays to view the house as a long term financial investment, not just a place to live.*
- *The net impact of saving small amounts through effective borrowing can create a great deal of future wealth.*
- *The shorter the time frame of house ownership, the greater the market risk from interest rate or valuation changes. Waiting to buy a house can be very costly in a rising real estate market, but buying a house too soon can be very costly if the market falls.*
- *One key approach to building wealth is to take any savings found from managing liabilities and use it to increase your assets.*

Chapter 2

Location, Location, Location

"We're not lost. We're locationally challenged." -- *John M. Ford*

If you were asked how the investment in your house compares to a 401(k), a checking account, an insurance policy, cash in a sock drawer, stocks, and stock or bond mutual funds, could you explain the difference? How can you compare your house with other investment products?

A financial advisor would seek to balance your tolerance for risk by selecting different investment products based on your desire for Safety, Liquidity, and Return. You can use those same three criteria to help understand the investment in your house. Additionally, to fully understand how the house compares, you should consider the house relative to taxes, leverage and diversification.

What we must consider, is that cash flowing into our lives can be used in one of three (3) ways; spending on current lifestyle, saving for a future lifestyle, or repayment of current outstanding debts.

Dispatching Your Wealth

The checking account is a transit hub for your income. New income immediately increases your net worth as it is a new asset on your balance sheet. As new wealth is dispatched to pay your bills for your current lifestyle, your net worth decreases. Any money left over at the end of the month can then be allocated toward specific savings (assets) or specific borrowing (liabilities). Net worth is your assets minus your liabilities.

Assets	-	Liabilities	=	Net Worth

Whenever you relocate funds from your checking account, it is a balance sheet neutral decision. It has no immediate impact on your net worth. You don't create new wealth when you dispatch money to your savings or to pay down your liabilities. The wealth in your checking account is already reflected in your net worth, as an asset.

A Sample Balance Sheet			
Assets		Liabilities	
Checking	$10,000	Mortgage	$160,000
Savings	$15,000	Auto Loans	$35,000
Investments	$175,000	Credit Cards	$5,000
House	$200,000		
Total	$400,000	Total	$200,000

In the above sample balance sheet, the net worth is $200,000, and $10,000 was left in checking at the end of the month. Should there be a move of $5,000 from the checking account to the investment account, the net worth remains the same. Money was simply moved from one asset to another. When you move assets from one asset to another, it is like moving money from your front pocket to your back pocket.

Moving $5,000 From Asset to Asset			
Assets		Liabilities	
Checking	$5,000	Mortgage	$160,000
Savings	$15,000	Auto Loans	$35,000
Investments	$180,000	Credit Cards	$5,000
House	$200,000		
Total	$400,000	Total	$200,000

Should there be a move of $5,000 from the checking account to the credit cards, the net worth remains the same. Even when money crosses the balance sheet, from an asset to a liability, the net worth remains the same. When you move an asset to a repay a liability, it is like moving money from your pocket to someone else's pocket.

Moving $5,000 From Asset to Liability			
Assets		Liabilities	
Checking	$5,000	Mortgage	$160,000
Savings	$15,000	Auto Loans	$35,000
Investments	$175,000	Credit Cards	$0
House	$200,000		
Total	$395,000	Total	$195,000

While the immediate decision to move money around on the balance sheet has no immediate visible impact, the long-term consequences of your decisions about the location of wealth are another matter. These decisions will only be realized later. Many of us come to learn that financial problems, like interest, compound over time. A small leak in the pipes may not become apparent until it requires a great deal of energy (time and money) to resolve. In essence, we want to find any financial leaks now

before they become a bigger problem later.
You probably understand that leaving your money in a checking account is not the best place to hold your long-term wealth. Why? At a basic level we know that there is an opportunity cost of leaving that money there based on other possible uses. The decision to relocate that money is sophisticated, whether you realize it or not. That money in the checking account was safe (guaranteed by the FDIC), it was liquid (you had complete use and control) and it was earning a Return (varies with banking institution). When the money is relocated to a person, company, or government, we understand that regardless of whatever benefits we receive, we've lost other possible uses of that money.

- *Relocate your checking account to a savings or money market account. The Safety and Liquidity is almost identical, but interest paid is often 3 or 4 times higher. Compare rates at www.bankrate.com.*

Throughout this book we'll consider in detail how this location of wealth relates to the house. When you invest in liabilities, this is typically done by paying off outstanding auto, credit card, student, mortgage, personal or business debt. When you invest in assets, this is typically done through financial products (savings accounts, CDs, money market funds, bonds, life insurance, stocks, annuities and mutual funds). Each location, whether an asset or a liability, has by its very nature aspects of Safety, Liquidity, and Return that can be measured.

When investing in assets or liabilities, you typically want the highest possible Safety (lowest risk of losing money), the highest Liquidity (highest use and control of your money), and the highest Return (highest earnings on your money). As you invest over time, you learn that there are gives and takes required to balance your ideal mix of Safety, Liquidity and Return based on your current specific goals and long-term financial needs.

Many of us pay a lot of attention to asset-oriented investments and receive a great deal of advice and information pertaining to asset products. Typically, we focus much less attention on the decisions related to our liabilities. Most of us have a choice of two different types of liabilities where we can locate our money: personal debt and investment debt.

Personal Debt

Personal debt is money borrowed to purchase an asset that will most likely depreciate in value. It is the most costly type of debt a person can have, because the asset will eventually depreciate to $0. If you borrow $30,000 at 6% interest to buy a new auto, what will it actually cost you? Your car payment of $579.88 over five years will return the $30,000 you borrowed with $4,799 in interest. At the end of five years, the car may be worth $10,000. Your investment of $34,799, less the car's five-year value of $10,000 would result in a net cost of $24,799.

Other types of personal debt include most credit card purchases, personal loans, and other unsecured debts used to invest in an asset that will depreciate in value. Because this debt is typically for something that will decrease in value, it is unsecured debt, so it will also require a higher interest rate.

Investment Debt

Investment debt is money borrowed to buy something that will typically hold or even appreciate in value. Although we refer to this as a form of debt, it often increases a person's net wealth. For example, consider the purchase of a house for $200,000 with a 30-year mortgage of $160,000 at a 6% interest rate. If the house itself were to appreciate at 3% per year, it would be worth $491,902 in 30 years. The interest you pay during this 30-year period would add up to $185,341. Thus, your payment for the house ($200,000) plus interest ($185,341) would total $385,341. However, you would have a house worth $491,902. Thus, you would gain $106,561 in future wealth related to this debt, not adjusting for inflation. Borrowing to start a new business would also fall into the investment debt category, as it has the potential to provide you a future asset that is worth a great deal more than what you borrowed to start the business.

Investment Assets

The alternative to investing in debt is investing in an asset. This is typically done by selecting a specific investment product. When you buy an investment product you are loaning the use of money you do not need today to someone else, providing them use and control of that money in exchange for gain through direct interest, dividends, or appreciation.

When you invest in liabilities you are repaying money that you have borrowed from others. When you invest in assets, you are allowing others to borrow from you – they are borrowing the use and control of your money. In other words, when you invest in an asset, you are letting someone else use your money, based on an expectation that the money will be there for you in the future (Safety), when you want or need it (Liquidity) and with increased buying power (Return). Understanding that basic concept can have a lifelong impact on your ability to create wealth.

Investing in Assets Versus Debts

When you pay off a debt or invest in an asset, it is crucial that you understand its impact on your total wealth over time.

If you have a $3,000 credit card balance with interest at 12.49%, you have borrowed money from a company that will receive a 12.49% Return from you. When you pay off that investment debt, you are making a debt investment that you can view through the lens of Safety, Liquidity, and Return.

The Safety of an investment in credit card debt is high, because there is little risk of losing money. If you write a check for $3,000 to pay off a $3,000 credit card debt, you can be sure that your new balance will be $0.

The Liquidity of paying off credit card debt is also high. Liquidity involves the use and control of your investment. Paying off the personal debt does not eliminate your use and control of the $3,000; you still have access to the money should you use the credit card for 'convenience'.

The Return on an investment in personal debt is also high. Your Return on the investment in your credit card debt would be 12.49%.

The following chart helps compare hypothetical investments in personal debt, investment debt, and investment assets. Remember, the Return on a personal or investment debt is the interest you are paying for money you borrow. The Return on an investment asset is what you earn for allowing others the use and control of your money.

Class	Type	Safety	Liquidity	Return	Rate
Personal Debt	credit card	high	high	high	18%
	personal loan	high	low	high	12%
	unsecured loan	high	low	high	10%
	car loan	high	low	medium	8%
Investment Debt	house mortgage	medium	medium	medium	6%
	student loan	high	low	low	4%
Investment Asset	mattress	medium	high	low	0%
	money market	high	high	low	1%
	CD	high	medium	low	2%
	bond	medium	high	low	4%
	insurance	medium	medium	medium	6%
	moderate stock	medium		medium	8%
	aggressive stock	low	medium	high	10%
	real estate	medium	low	high	12%
	loan shark	low	low	high	18%

**these rates are hypothetical*

This book will help you think clearly and confidently when faced with a decision about investing in debts or assets. Any time you have money available, you face an investment decision. Whether you save $100 each month, receive $2,000 from a tax refund, gain $50,000 from the sale of a house, or earn $500,000 from the sale of a business, you need to decide where to locate your money. The above chart provides a general comparison of a few of the many products available.

The decision to locate wealth inside the house is a unique investment product consideration. For most Americans, the house represents a person's largest single asset (% of net worth) while also representing the largest single debt (% of monthly expense). Therefore, management of the house asset and mortgage debt can have a huge impact on one's ability to create wealth over time.

No other single investment asset or debt is as misunderstood as the house. If you own your house free and clear, it could still be costing you a great deal of money. If you own your house with a mortgage, you could be focusing too much of your investment savings toward the repayment of your mortgage debt, or leaving too much in CDs or savings accounts that could have repaid debt. The house is a wonderful investment, but like any investment, it needs to be approached from the perspective of Safety, Liquidity and Return.

If you pick dates for a one-week family vacation, would that vacation be relaxing and enjoyable if you packed up the car and drove to the airport with no flight reservations, planning the trip as you went? A successful vacation is often the by product of careful planning to arrange crucial details and reservations so that you will have the freedom to simply enjoy yourself along the way.

When you are buying or refinancing a house, there are so many details and considerations involved that it's hard to focus on wealth creation. However, taking time to plan this important financial move is well worth the effort. Working with a lender, financial advisor, Realtor®—or all three—helps put maximum wealth creation within your reach. Not doing so can have expensive hidden costs that compound later in life.

Even without much planning, owning a house over an extended period of time is usually more lucrative than renting. With good planning and execution, you can learn to minimize the cost of house ownership, while maximizing your ability to create real wealth. Ultimately the decision of where you locate your wealth (location, location, location) is one of the most important decisions you can make.

Summary of Key Learnings

- *All things being equal, look for the highest possible Safety, Liquidity, and Return when making an investment.*

- *Personal debt is money borrowed for depreciating assets. The decreasing value in the underlying assets raises the cost of the debt.*

- *Investment debt is money borrowed for appreciating assets. The increasing value in the underlying assets reduces the cost of the debt. It may even create new wealth.*

- *Money in investment assets is money loaned to others for their use and control. The goal is for the money to increase in future buying power.*

- *It can be hard to determine whether to pay off investment debt or increase investment assets. Both may be similar in Safety, Liquidity, and Return.*

Chapter 3

Safety

"Safe upon the solid rock the ugly houses stand: Come and see my shining palace built upon the sand!" -- Edna St. Vincent Millay

If you are going to work with a power tool, understand how to safely operate it first, then you can begin using it in a variety of ways. Financial tools can also be very powerful, but it pays to use them with a "safety first" approach.

Will Rogers once said, "Return 'of' my money is more important than return 'on' my money." If you don't want to lose the money you invest in a house, it is helpful to understand the key risks to a house investment. How comfortable are you with the prospect of losing some or all of the investment in your house? How much volatility are you comfortable with in the value of the house?

Safety can be defined in many ways, but we'll define Safety as minimizing the potential loss of the investment you make.

A Hypothetical House Purchase

Imagine that you are purchasing a $200,000 house with a $40,000 down payment and a $160,000 mortgage for 30 years at 6%.

- *To control real estate worth $200,000 (investment asset), you have relocated $40,000 (investment asset) to the seller and borrowed $160,000 (investment debt) from the lender, but the $40,000 (investment asset) is also collateral to the lender.*

Let's also assume that your $200,000 house appreciates at 3% each year. We will use this example to help illustrate the possible risks in a house investment. Any of these numbers could vary, but even if the down payment, the amount and type of mortgage, and the appreciation or depreciation percentages are different, the risk concepts involved would be similar.

In the case of the $200,000 house, in what ways is your $40,000 down payment at risk? To minimize the potential loss of the wealth in your house, you need to understand the "threats" that could lead to a loss of some or all of your $40,000.

There are four primary risks that could become threats to the wealth in your house: appreciation, depreciation, foreclosure and lawsuit.

Wealth in the House

If you own a house, your wealth in the house is constantly changing in accordance with the amount of principal paid monthly and fluctuations in the value of the house. How can you prepare for dramatic changes in the value of your house? How is the wealth in your house at risk when the value of the house decreases?

There are two important concepts to consider related to appreciation and depreciation of a house:

1) Appreciation and depreciation are influenced by the general market

conditions at a state and national level, as well as local market conditions at a county, city, and neighborhood level. Of course, the overall condition and appearance of a house also affects its value.

2) The market is always "right." In other words, a buyer has overriding influence on the value of a house in terms of what he or she is willing to pay for the house relevant to the market as a whole.

If the average price for a house in your local area rises from $125 to $150 per square foot, that should help boost the appreciation of your house. If the general market shows a downward movement from $125 to $100 per square foot, you could see a general downward movement in the appreciation of your house. That much seems obvious.

If you make an investment in a large company traded on the stock exchange and the overall stock market improves, you might expect your stock to improve as well, while a downward trend in the overall stock market might lead to a decrease in the value of your stock. Individually, the stock still trades on its own merits, and positive or negative news about the company will likely influence the stock value independently of the larger market.

Similarly, various factors beyond the individual house influence changes in its value. An attractive neighborhood, ongoing maintenance, renovations, local amenities, transportation, and the quality of local schools all affect the appreciation or depreciation of a house. Your house is part of a general housing market and also a subset of the local housing market. If the market as a whole is rising or falling, it will influence the value of your house in ways over which you may have little control. You may be out of luck if a local employer has massive layoffs, a nearby lake becomes contaminated, your school district changes, or a new highway cuts through the neighborhood.

Ultimately, however, the value of a house remains in the eye of the beholder—the buyer. That is why we say, "The market is always right." The buyer and the seller negotiate the final price of a house. The general market valuation helps determine the overall value to a point, but the amount that an individual buyer is willing to pay can make a huge difference in the price.

If you live in a great neighborhood but your house is in need of repair, you'll see a drag on the overall market appreciation. An individual buyer might like your house location so much, however, that he or she is willing to pay more for your house than for a similar house in better condition and a less favorable location. That is one reason we often hear that real estate is ultimately about location, location, location.

The U.S. housing market went through a period of unprecedented appreciation, driven by low interest rates, easy to borrow loan products, and high consumer demand. That convergence of influences drove house prices to all-time highs. Then, risky leveraged investments in those same mortgage products, created a global stock market meltdown that took housing prices on their most dramatic historic drop of our lifetime.

It's hard to predict what real estate value will do next. Historically the riskiest time to buy an asset is at an all time high, and the least risky time to buy an asset is at an all time low. House prices could go lower, but how much lower? Interest rates can go lower, but how much lower? It's best to think in terms of probabilities. Is it more probably that things go higher, or lower from where we are today?

A typical investment product, such as a mutual fund, provides some relative measure of Safety, Liquidity and Return. If you find that a mutual fund isn't meeting your desired mix of Safety, Liquidity or Return, you can sell it, and invest in something more suitable to your current needs. If your house isn't meeting your needs for Safety, Liquidity, or Return, it isn't quite so simple. The decision to sell your house and move, can be a life-changing decision. Selling a house takes much longer than selling a mutual fund, and it is far more disruptive. The 'home' and impact to family often overrides the financial impact of the house. Proper planning can help you manage threats to maximize financial housing flexibility, and minimize family disruptions that impact your experience of home.

The Appreciation Threat

How can appreciation be a "threat?" Rapid appreciation often results in higher property taxes and higher insurance premiums. Such increases may burden the house owner without providing any realized financial benefits. A house owner seeking merely to stay in their house may need to utilize wealth inside the house to support increasing costs.

If a house owner is not managing the wealth in the house, an increase in valuation can seem like a nuisance expense. In fact, rising house values increase the need for effective management of the growing wealth inside the house to support the higher expenses associated with real estate taxes and insurance. Many retired people living on fixed incomes end up selling their houses because they feel overwhelmed by fast-rising property taxes.

Many who have seen rapid house appreciation have cashed out wealth from their house to support a variety of different expenses. Access to the wealth through equity lines of credit, debit cards, cash out refinances, and reverse mortgages can help make house equity available to support higher costs stemming from the appreciation threat.

The Depreciation Threat

A second key threat to wealth in the house could come through market depreciation. Since the 2006 top, house prices have dropped from 18% to 65% in value depending on your market.

Returning to our earlier example, imagine that your $200,000 house was purchased in 1996. Imagine that it appreciated at 4% annually for five years, to a value of $244,199. Then, over the next five years, it depreciated 23% to $184,614. After ten years, your house would be worth $15,386 less than the $200,000 you paid for it originally. If a job or other pressures forced you to move during a period of market depreciation, you might be lucky to get $179,000. After paying a 6% Realtor commission you'd receive a check for $168,260. Thus, the house investment would have decreased your net worth by $31,740 over 10 years. If the net payment is lower than your mortgage balance, you'll have to write a check to be able to move.

Losses occur only when you must sell a property during a market downturn. To reduce the threat of depreciation to your house, you need to be able to control the timing of the sale.

- *Market appreciation and depreciation are functions of broader market movements, the local market, and the individual property.*
- *The key to avoiding loss of wealth in a depreciating market is having the flexibility to wait for the market to recover.*

Protecting Against Depreciation

How might you have increased the Safety of the wealth in your house? If you are able to stay in your house for some time, you may well be able to ride out a depressed market. In Houston, in 1978, a 23% decrease in property values took only 5 year to recover from as the economy picked up and interest rates remained low. The key to avoiding a loss on real estate depreciation lies in your ability to control the timing of the sale. Historically, since the 1800's, the demand for housing has always led to a market recovery in valuation. On average it's taken from as little as 3 to as many as 10 years, depending on the amount of the depreciation, the size of the market, and other factors.

If you must move to another area and sell at a reduced price—if you have no better option—then you must accept the loss and start over in your new locality, hoping that your loss as a seller will allow you to also buy low as a new buyer. If you have more flexibility, however, you might, for example, move to another city and keep the old house as a rental until the market recovers. That way, you might be able to turn a loss into a gain, buying your new house low, and selling the old house higher. One strategy to protect against a timing loss, is an equity line of credit.

Depreciation Example

Imagine this scenario: twin brothers, Tom and Bill, age 35, each purchase a house for $200,000 in a Houston neighborhood in 1978. Each puts down $40,000 and borrows $160,000 on a 30-year fixed-rate mortgage at 7%. They both live in the same neighborhood and work together at the same company. The company ceases operation in 1988.

Tom and Bill both see 4% annual appreciation on their houses for five years. In 1983, their company begins to struggle and lays off a number of workers, who are forced to sell their houses and relocate to other job markets. During the five-year period from 1983 to 1988, Tom and Bill each experience a 23% drop in his house value. When the company ceases operations in 1988, both brothers are able to find work in Dallas.

In 1988, when Tom and Bill both moved to Dallas with their families, Tom is forced to sell his house, suffering a $15,386 loss. Bill manages to keep his house for another five years, and in 1993, he sells it for a $25,485 profit.

Twin Brothers (Age 35)				
$200,000 house • $160,000 mortgage • $40,000 initial investment				
	Year 0	Years 1-5	Years 6-10	Years 11-15
Age	35	40	45	50
Appreciation	0%	20%	-23%	20%
House Value	$200,000	$244,199	$184,614	$225,485
Net Equity	$40,000	$84,199	$24,614	$65,485
			Tom Sells	Bill Sells
Difference: $65,485 - $24,614 =				$40,871

Tom sells because he needs the money from his Houston house to make a down payment on a new house in Dallas. For six months, he lists the house for sale in Houston and rents a house in Dallas.

Bill, however, having taken precautions to protect the wealth in his house, has set up an equity line of credit. He uses $25,000 of the equity in his Houston house to purchase a new house in Dallas. For the next five years, he is able to rent out the Houston house for enough to cover his mortgage payments on the Dallas house. In other words, he manages his house wealth to make sure he has access in various situations.

From this example, you can see how important it can be to control the timing of a house sale in order to protect the wealth in the house from depreciation. The best way to maximize flexibility is to have access to the wealth in the house when you need it.

Impact on Wealth

Continuing with the story of Tom and Bill: both brothers plan to retire at age 65. Tom receives $24,614 from the sale of his house, a $15,386 loss of his original $40,000 investment. He uses it as a down payment to buy a new house in Dallas.

Bill sells his house to his renters, receiving $65,484 five years later. He is able to pay off his $25,000 home equity line of credit and put $40,000 into his investment portfolio. Since he bought the Houston house at age 35 and sold it 15 years later, he gains $40,000 to invest at age 50 - fifteen years before retirement. If he were to invest $40,000 at 6% (after taxes) for 15 years, it would grow to $98,376 by age 65, giving him more than enough to pay off his remaining mortgage on the house he purchased when he moved to Dallas.

- *Avoiding a loss from market depreciation is crucial to protecting future wealth.*

The Foreclosure Threat

The third key threat to wealth in the house is Foreclosure. If you cannot make your mortgage payments and a lender forecloses, you lose control of the house. You also lose control of the wealth in the house. The lender sells the house to recover the outstanding loan. The selling price usually begins at the current loan balance, with no guarantee that your net equity will be returned. A surprisingly large number of people have lost a house through foreclosure. Most people believe it could never happen to them. How could it possibly happen to you?

In most states there is a contract (or note) and a deed with every house purchase. The deed records who owns the house (typically the buyer), and who owns the wealth (typically the buyer). The bank is rarely on the deed, they have no ownership in your property. The contract explains the terms under which the buyer has borrowed the money. In our example of the $200,000 house, the contract would clarify that you are borrowing $160,000 for 30 years at 6%. The contract would also give payment due dates, specifying, for example, that your mortgage payment is due on the first day of each month, and that payments received after the 15th day of the month are subject to a penalty. It would also say that payments not received by the 30th of the month are "late," subjecting you to credit damage. The process of foreclosure might begin on the 60th day after the due date.

For your hypothetical $160,000 mortgage, the bank provides money for your purchase of the property. The property remains collateral as a guarantee to the bank for as long as your balance is greater than $0. The contract dictates the terms of repayment required for you to stay in control of the deed. If you fail to honor the terms of the contract, you can lose control of the deed through the process of foreclosure. The lender then replaces you as the controlling owner and sells the deed (control of the house) to a third party.

No one who invests money in a house plans to go into foreclosure, yet foreclosure is increasingly common. The majority of those house owners probably felt their wealth could be invested in nothing safer than a house when they purchased it.

- *When you borrow money for a house, you have a contract and a deed. The contract determines who owns the deed.*

- *The deed controls the ownership of the house and the wealth inside the house.*

Lose control of the deed, and you lose control of the wealth still inside the house.

A Prepayment Scenario

Let's continue the example of your $40,000 investment in a $200,000 house with a $160,000 mortgage at 6% amortizing over 30 years. Your monthly payment for principal and interest is $959.

Imagine that after 12 months your rich uncle dies and you receive an inheritance of $60,000. Your net worth increases immediately as you deposit the proceeds in your checking account as a new asset.

After Inheritance of $60,000			
Assets		**Liabilities**	
Checking	**$70,000**	Mortgage	$160,000
Savings	$15,000	Auto Loans	$35,000
Investments	$175,000	Credit Cards	$5,000
House	$200,000		
Total	**$460,000**	**Total**	**$200,000**
$460,000 - $200,000 = $260,000 (net worth)			

You decide you want the security of owning your house free and clear as quickly as possible, so you apply the entire sum to your mortgage. For your next payment, you send the lender $60,959. You have chosen to locate (invest) your $60,000 inheritance in an investment debt, which will reduce the interest due on your house debt by $60,000. Your mortgage balance of $160,000 shrinks immediately to $100,000. Your net worth remains the same, because the decision of where to locate wealth after you deposit it in your checking account is initially a balance sheet neutral decision.

After Mortgage Prepayment of $60,000			
Assets		**Liabilities**	
Checking	**$10,000**	Mortgage	**$100,000**
Savings	$15,000	Auto Loans	$35,000
Investments	$175,000	Credit Cards	$5,000
House	$200,000		
Total	**$400,000**	**Total**	**$140,000**
$400,000 - $140,000 = $260,000 (net worth)			

Your contract on the 30-year fixed mortgage shows a $959 payment due the first of each month until the mortgage balance is zero. Since the $60,000 prepayment does not bring your balance to zero, the full payment of $959 is still due in full on the first of each month. Your $60,000 payment reduces the amount of interest you owe, so your next payment of $959 will include less interest and more principal. Your $60,000 payment will end up reducing the remaining term of your mortgage from 29 years to 11 years. For the next 11 years, the lender has the use of your $60,000.

Now imagine that a year later you lose your job. You invested $60,000 to lower your mortgage to $100,000 from the original $160,000, but the payment of $959 is still due each month. If you can't make the payment for two consecutive months, you could be faced with a foreclosure process and a future loss of the control of the deed, and subsequently the wealth in the house. The house now has your original $40,000 investment, plus $60,000 from the inheritance. Therefore, you have $100,000 at risk in the event of a Foreclosure, and the lender has $100,000 in collateral, not just the original $40,000. The potential threat of foreclosure remains until you pay the entire mortgage balance.

- *Paying a lump sum on a fixed-rate mortgage will not reduce your monthly mortgage payment.*

- *Additional wealth invested to pay down a mortgage provides additional security to the lender, not to the borrower.*

- *Additional wealth invested to pay down a mortgage reduces the interest expense and the remaining term of the loan.*

- *Wealth in a house is not guaranteed. If you become unable to make payments, the lender can exercise its contractual right to take possession of the deed and sell the house.*

Protecting Against Foreclosure

The unforeseen experience of foreclosure can happen in many different ways. The majority of the events that lead to foreclosure are largely beyond our control. These include disability, loss of employment, divorce, and death.

Key Foreclosure Threats	
Disability	Loss Of Job
Divorce	Death

If you prepay a partial extra payment of $60,000 on an amortizing mortgage, your next full payment is still due the following month. Your monthly payment would only decrease if you were to refinance, or if your mortgage is a special type that constantly adjusts the next payment to your current loan balance.

With an amortizing fixed mortgage your payments typically stay the same until you make your final payment. Even with an adjustable-rate mortgage, you will see no adjustment in the amount due until the fixed portion of the interest rate expires and the loan adjusts to a new payment based on a new rate and the current balance.

You probably have friends who have been divorced or disabled, had a spouse die, or lost a job unexpectedly. Maybe you know a Hurricane Katrina victim who lost his or her house. Think about the odds of an unforeseen occurrence that could lead to major financial hardship. Prepaying a mortgage can be financially hazardous in any of those situations.

Without proper planning, paying down a mortgage without paying it off in full can lead to a false sense of security. By examining the events that often lead to foreclosure, we can create a strategy to protect the wealth in the house from this threat. If you have access to the wealth in your house, you could use it to help protect the house from foreclosure. The goal is to find a way to make the wealth in the house available in the case of a foreclosure.

The Lawsuit Threat

The fourth key threat to wealth in the house could come from a lawsuit or related legal threat, such as bankruptcy. If you live in FL, IA, KS, SD, OK, DC, or TX the homestead exemption act provides unlimited protection of wealth in the house from most lawsuits and bankruptcy acts. If you live in AZ, MA, MN, NV, or RI your exemptions are for equity above $100,000. Those living in other states are at a greater risk from a legal threats or actions that might seek to access wealth inside your house.

There are two primary ways to reduce the likelihood of a lawsuit. First, the house could be inside an LLC to insulate the risk from any personal lawsuit, or to protect from a personal lawsuit. The problem with LLC ownership involves the loss of Schedule A tax deductions, the loss of *gain on sale* provisions allowed for a house owned by the seller for 2 of the last 5 years, or other due on sale clauses that might be triggered. The second deterrent would be to have no wealth inside the house, eliminating the house as a potential asset for lawsuit. To do this, wealth inside the house would need to be repositioned to specific products (life insurance, annuities, etc.) that are secure from creditors / predators, or into a separate LLC or Limited Partnership. This must be done before any known action, or pending threat of litigation has occurred.

If your concern is purely Safety from lawsuit or potential bankruptcy, be careful transferring assets outside the house if you are in a state that protects house wealth, as you could take an asset that was otherwise protected, and place it at risk.

While a house is generally considered a safe investment, it is not a guaranteed investment. Without proper planning, you could lose wealth through depreciation, foreclosure or lawsuit. In our 7–Step Solution, we'll discuss a strategy you can use to increase the Safety of the wealth in your house from all four of these possible threats.

Summary of Key Learnings

- The two biggest threats to the Safety of wealth in the house are depreciation and foreclosure.
- House appreciation and depreciation are influenced by broad market movements and by individual buyers.
- The market and the individual buyer are always right.
- The key to avoiding loss of wealth in a depreciating real estate market is to have the flexibility to wait for the market to recover.
- A single large loss from market depreciation can result in a substantial loss of future wealth.
- When you borrow money for a house, you have a contract and a deed. The contract determines who controls the deed.
- Pre-paying a lump sum on a fixed-rate mortgage will not reduce the amount of your monthly mortgage payment.
- Additional wealth invested to pay down a mortgage provides additional security to the lender, not to the owner.
- Your wealth in your house is not guaranteed. If you were unable to make payments, the bank could exercise its contractual right to take possession of the deed.

Chapter 4

Liquidity

"It is the city of mirrors, the city of mirages, at once solid and liquid, at once air and stone." -- *Erica Jong*

If you have money in a 401(k) or IRA, you probably view it differently from your other investments. You know it is your money, but you also know there are conditions that regulate your ability to access that money, including how and when you spend it.

Investment products have different degrees of Liquidity for different reasons. The government provides tax benefits as an enticement to invest in "qualified" retirement plans. The bank offers a higher rate on a CD than for a checking or savings account. A lender may offer a reduced rate for a prepayment penalty. In each of these cases, an institution is seeking to limit use and control for its own purposes.

We'll define Liquidity as the speed and ease with which you may convert your wealth to cash. If you pay $200,000 in cash for a house, you have use and control of the house, but you give up the use and control of $200,000. Your $200,000 is now inside the house.

"Money in the house" is house equity. Positive or negative house equity impacts your net worth. That said, there is no real money in the house. The house has value. The value that exceeds any current borrowing is positive equity, the value that is below any current borrowing is negative equity.

Suppose that instead of paying cash, you kept your $200,000 in cash and took out a $200,000 mortgage loan to buy the house. You would have use and control of the $200,000. You would then make monthly interest payments for the use and control of the house to the bank.

Lenders are willing to lend against the house value for several reasons:

- *They can make a profit.*
- *They believe you can and will repay the money.*
- *They expect the house value to increase or at least hold value.*

Your ability to convert that value of the house to cash in the future is the degree of Liquidity of your house equity based on what a lender will lend against the property. Your individual Liquidity of the wealth in your house is relative to your individual strength as a borrower. Both of these have to work together for you to borrow.

Why Borrow Money?

There may be many reasons that you choose not to borrow money, but there are only two reasons to borrow money: (1) you need to, or (2) you choose to.

If you want to buy a house for $200,000 and you have $40,000 to invest, you must borrow at least $160,000 to complete the transaction. Debt is necessary. You are a debtor.

If you want to buy a house for $200,000 and you have $200,000 to invest, you could buy the house without borrowing. Or, you could invest $40,000 into the house and borrow $160,000. You are still a debtor, but the debt is optional. You have the opportunity to act as a creditor.

A debtor borrows money out of necessity. A creditor is a debtor who borrows money based on financial opportunity. Whatever your situation today, it will pay to understand and maximize your ability to use Liquidity to create new wealth. Smart borrowing can help you move more quickly from borrowing out of necessity - to borrowing out of choice. If you are already borrowing based solely on opportunity, smart borrowing can help you further amplify your future wealth.

Accessing House Wealth

There are only two ways to convert the wealth in a house to cash: sell the house, or borrow against the house. Selling the house provides complete use and control of the cash, but one loses the use and control of the house. Borrowing against the house provides complete use and control of the cash *and* complete use and control of the house as long as one makes monthly interest payments on the debt. Let's compare the Liquidity of house equity to other investments.

Investment	**Time To Convert To Cash**		
	<30 days	**45-60 days**	**>60 days**
cash	**X**		
bonds	**X**		
stocks	**X**		
House Equity	**<30 days**	**45-60 days**	**>60 days**
equity line	**X***		
cash out refinance		**X***	
house sale			**X**
*assumes you can qualify to borrow			

1. House Sale

When you sell a house, you end up trading the use and control of the house for cash. To list, market, sell, finance, move, and close on a house with usable cash in hand might take 60 days to a year, depending on market timing and the condition and location of the house.

How soon you need to convert the house to cash may affect the amount of cash you receive. If you need to complete the process quickly, you may sell it at a lower price. The cash (net equity) you receive is typically the selling price at closing minus real estate commissions, fees, and any outstanding borrowing secured by the property.

2. Borrowing against the House

Imagine that you are living in a house, and you want to convert your house equity into cash while maintaining ownership. Your best bet would be to borrow against the value of the house. Any borrowing against the house will be based on the appraised value of the house at the time you borrow.

There are several different ways to borrow against the value of a house. You can use a first mortgage, an equity line of credit, or a second mortgage. If you are at a qualifying age, you could also use a reverse mortgage.

No matter how you borrow against the value of a house, you will use the house as collateral. With most financing options, the process of converting the value of the house to cash takes about 45 to 60 days. The timing depends on market conditions for application, processing, appraisal, approval, and closing.

To better understand the Safety of the wealth in the house, we looked at the two key threats to the wealth: depreciation and foreclosure. To understand the Liquidity of the wealth in the house, we examine the four primary obstacles to converting the wealth in the house to cash through borrowing.

Obstacles to Borrowing

Borrowing is always subject to the guidelines and eligibility requirements set by the lender. The rules governing how and when you are eligible to access money through borrowing change frequently based on various agency guidelines, market conditions, interest rates, market capacity, and other factors. Once a loan has closed, however, the repayment terms are reflected in a written contract between you and the lender.

Typically, a borrower must overcome four key eligibility obstacles to convert house equity to cash through borrowing. In the lending business we call these obstacles the four C's: Character, Capacity, Collateral, and Credit.

Four Obstacles to Borrowing	
Character	Capacity
Collateral	Credit

Each of the four C's has some sub elements, but there is one chief obstacle associated with each. Most people learn about these obstacles by running into them at full speed while in the middle of trying to borrow against the value of the house for a specific need. This is probably the most painful way to learn a lesson in Liquidity.

Let's explore the four obstacles and look at the chief obstacle associated with each.

Obstacle 1 - Character

Your "Character" on a loan application includes your rental history, the number of years you have owned a house, your marital status, the number of children you have and their ages, your employment history, any lawsuits you have been involved in, back taxes owed, and other personal and financial matters.

The key obstacle related to Character eligibility relates to your current and future ability to repay the debt. Remember, the lender wants a predictable payment stream from you each month. A lender will believe you are more likely to make monthly payments if you can show your ability to earn steady income in a career. To meet the primary Character obstacle, you want to be able to provide at least a two-year employment history in a particular profession or line of work.

Consider this example: A high school teacher leaves after 15 years to study and become a contractor. He studies during the summer, successfully secures his contractor license, and decides to build a house. To finance it, he decides to use wealth in the house he already owns. He meets with a lender to set up an equity line of credit.

Since he has no history of earning income as a contractor, the lender will probably not provide a loan against his house. The lender would prefer not to risk the loan without a history of the borrower earning income as a contractor. Had he understood this while he was still a teacher, he could have set up an equity line of credit before making the career change.

I have spoken with hundreds of prospective borrowers who believed the value of their house would be there for the asking – only to realize that a career change, retirement, or other major change caused them to fail the "Character" test for accessing the wealth in their house.

- *Before retiring or making a career change, you should set up access to wealth you expect to need from the house.*

- *The primary obstacle for Character is a job history of two or more years in the same line of work or profession.*

Obstacle 2 - Capacity

Most of the second page of a standard loan application focuses on Capacity, which pertains to income from jobs and investments. Maybe you've heard the old saying, "Cash is king." Unless you can pay cash in full for a property, however, *cash flow* is king.

Most debts have a monthly balance and monthly payments, either contractually with the same amount due each month (as in a car payment), or contractually with a percentage due each month (as in a credit card payment). The lender wants to know that your income will exceed your debts, as they are counting on your income stream to support their needs as a lender. Essentially, will you will keep your promise to repay your debts.

The key obstacle to Capacity relates to a specific ratio of debt to income. Lenders use a Capacity guideline which requires that you have income to cover your mortgage liability and your other liabilities based on a certain ratio. A common guideline ratio used by lenders is 28/36.

The top number is the percentage of income available for mortgage loan repayment. With a 28/36 ratio, your maximum monthly payment would be 28% of your monthly income. If you make $100,000 a year, 28% of that, or $28,000 ($2,333 per month) would be the most you could "afford" to pay for your mortgage loan, including taxes and insurance (assuming the lender holds tight to that guideline).

The bottom number is the percentage of your verifiable income that would have to be used to make all your debt payments in a timely manner. With a 28/36 ratio, your mortgage payment plus all other debts combined should not exceed 36% of your total gross income.

If you earn $100,000 a year, the 36% guideline would say that 36% of $100,000, or $36,000 ($3,000 per month) would be your maximum total monthly payments for your mortgage (including taxes and insurance), your car, credit cards, and any other debt payments, all combined.

You can see how interest rate fluctuations affect Capacity guidelines. If interest rates decrease, your payment will be a lower percentage of your total gross income, which could allow you to buy a more expensive house. As interest rates rise, a decreasing portion of the population can afford to buy a house, and fewer people can afford to enter the market.

A simple rule of thumb is that you can figure on borrowing up to four times your verified gross annual income. ("Verified" means income you report to the IRS.) For example, imagine that John and Mary Smith have a combined gross annual income of $100,000. Typically, they would qualify for a $400,000 mortgage if they have no liabilities (other debts). However, if their annual income is $50,000 and they own a house valued at $400,000, there is probably a Liquidity gap between the wealth in the house and the amount they can access based on Capacity.

Each lender uses its own criteria for loan approvals, but Capacity serves a role in determining how much the lender will allow you to borrow against the value in your house. Therefore, a rise or fall in your income affects your Liquidity.

Here is an example: John Smith earns $25,000 per year, and Mary Smith earns $75,000. John's income is barely enough to cover the couple's childcare expenses, so they decide that John will quit his job to stay home with the children full time. Their combined income of $100,000 had been enough to qualify them for the $400,000 mortgage on their house. A year after John quits his job, a health emergency requires extra cash, and the Smiths need access to wealth in their house. The Capacity obstacle would limit their ability to access the wealth in the house, since their income has decreased to $75,000. Their new borrowing maximum is lower than the amount they'd previously borrowed.

- *Any change to income or expenses will change your Capacity ratio, and increase or decrease your ability to convert your house value to cash.*

- *The key obstacle for Capacity is the ability to show income that will support the mortgage and debt payments at a ratio suitable to the lender.*

Obstacle 3 - Collateral

House Collateral is initially your down payment—the amount of money you invest in the house at the time of a purchase or refinance. Over time the Collateral grows as the house appreciates and you pay down the loan. In theory, the lenders House Collateral should increase each month over the life of the loan.

Lenders also consider Collateral outside the house—i.e., Collateral that is not tied to the house but that would support your ability to repay the loan. This is money you have available in your investments, non-qualified retirement accounts, checking and savings accounts, insurance cash value, and other liquid holdings. Collateral in the house and Collateral outside the house serve two different purposes.

The Collateral in the house protects the lender in the event of a negative event, like a foreclosure. Should you default on your payments, the process of foreclosure would give the lender use and control of the house and any Collateral in the house to reduce their losses. The lender could sell the house to recover its money loaned to you.

Collateral outside the house helps you maintain use and control of your house indirectly. You can use it if needed to make house payments. The lender likes to see that you have Collateral outside the house to weather any financial storms that might come your way. If you exhaust your external Collateral and stop making mortgage payments, the lender will look to Collateral in the house to resolve the shortcoming through the foreclosure process.

Thus, a lender will look first at your job stability (Character), then at your income (Capacity), and, thirdly, at your down payment or equity (Collateral inside the house). Your Collateral outside the house is discretionary savings that would support your ability to make your mortgage payments.

If there are gaps in your job history (Character) and your income (Capacity), then a lender might require additional Collateral inside the house (larger down payment) as a condition for loan approval. If you have great job history and great income, then a lender may require less Collateral inside the house. In that case, you would be free to decide how much to locate inside the house as a down payment.

Collateral in the house is more valuable to the lender. Collateral outside the house is more valuable to the borrower. If you were to default on your loan, the lender would have control over Collateral in the house. You and the lender share some of the same threats to Safety: (1) foreclosure (as the lender becomes the owner) if you are unable to make payments and (2) depreciation (the value of the lender's collateral decreases) increasing their risk if you default.

Lenders providing a Forward Mortgage look for balance among the C's. Having plenty of Collateral can help offset lack of Character and Capacity. High Character and Capacity ratings can help offset lack of Collateral inside the house. If you own a $200,000 house with no mortgage, and you need to convert 50% of the equity in the house into cash through a new mortgage you'll need a lender, and they'll look at all the C's to determine if they are willing to make you that loan. In some instances, like a Reverse Mortgage, the C (Collateral) is the primary focus, the other 3 C's are not as critical.

- *The Collateral inside the house protects the lender first, while the Collateral outside the house protects you first.*

- *The 4 C's can offset one another. Having plenty of Collateral can help offset lack of Character and Capacity. High Character and Capacity ratings can help offset lack of Collateral inside the house.*

- *The key obstacle for Collateral is a down payment located inside the house for direct security of the loan, or outside the house for reduced risk of default.*

While each of these three obstacles is important, the fourth obstacle, Credit, has become the most important single factor for Liquidity of wealth in the house.

Obstacle 4 - Credit

Your ability to repay mortgage debt on time is the lender's greatest single concern in approving a new mortgage loan or refinance. Credit is the greatest indicator of your ability and your willingness to repay in a timely manner.

The higher your Credit score, the lower the risk of payment default or delayed payment. Typical credit scores range from 400 to 900, with key milestones at 500, 620 and 740. The higher your score, the lower the statistical risk to the lender that you will not make your payment. The lower the risk, the lower the interest rate a lender may offer.

Credit measures your ability and willingness to repay your debts on time. Willingness is even more important than ability to repay, but both impact your Credit score. Many wealthy borrowers who have low Credit scores don't realize that making occasional late payments, over time, shows an unwillingness to pay in a timely manner. This can do great harm to their Credit. Someone with $1 million sitting in a checking account who forgets to pay on time can expect to receive the same Credit treatment as someone who has lost his or her job and missed a payment because he or she lacked the ability to pay on time.

Identity theft or a dramatic financial setback can also lower your Credit score enough to make borrowing difficult or impossible.

These days, it is more important than ever to monitor your Credit score on a regular basis if you want to borrow at the lowest possible interest. A good Credit rating helps maximize your use and control of the wealth in your house. High Credit scores translate to lower loan rates.

- *A decrease in your Credit score can be a primary obstacle to your use and control of the wealth in your house.*

- *Missed payments can hurt your Credit score over time.*

- *Identify theft or a dramatic financial setback can quickly reduce one's score to a level where borrowing is difficult or impossible.*

- *You should review your Credit score at least once a year.*

- *The key obstacle for Credit is a score that meets the minimum requirements of the lender.*

Chief Obstacles

If we look at life events that lead to a lack of Liquidity, we can focus on the four C's. The following is a list of common threats that can become obstacles to accessing wealth in the house.

Life Event*	Liquidity Obstacle:
Job Loss / Career Change	Character
Lawsuit Against You	
Forced Early Retirement	
Income Changes	Capacity
Disability	
Death	
House Value Changes	Collateral
Tax Lien	
Marriage / Divorce	
Identity Theft	Credit
Collection	
Judgment	

**some events impact several liquidity obstacles*

Ironically, many of these life events accompany an increased need for Liquidity. Events that make accessing the wealth in the house a priority make it more difficult to access this wealth. John F. Kennedy is famous for saying, "The best time to repair the roof is when the sun is still shining", but it is often the most difficult. Your ability to get access to the wealth in your house when you most need it is challenged by guidelines that are designed to prevent access to money in the event of financial hardship, for you or the lender, that would create more risk to the lender.

From the perspective of Liquidity (the speed at which you can convert the wealth in your house to cash) there are conditions governing when, how, and even how much of the wealth in the house you can convert to cash.

Wealth in the house is much less liquid than most other investments, and various life events can cause it to become totally illiquid. It is important to understand the obstacles to accessing that wealth for either necessity or opportunity.

The house is a safe investment, but not a guaranteed investment. The house is a Liquid investment, but the timing and conditions of selling the house, or borrowing against it, make the house one of your least Liquid investments.

Summary of Key Learnings

- *There are two ways to access wealth in the house: sell it, or borrow against it.*
- *The speed at which you can convert wealth in the house to cash can vary dramatically, depending on how you access the wealth.*
- *The life events that often increase the need for access to the wealth in your house are typically the same events that block such access.*

- *Any time you plan a career change or retirement, you should determine how much wealth you anticipate needing in the future and access that wealth before making the planned change.*

- *Character as an eligibility requirement deems it important to have a two-year job history for optimal financing.*

- *Any change to income or expenses will affect your Capacity ratio and increase or decrease your ability to use and control your wealth in the house.*

- *Capacity as an eligibility requirement deems it important that you show income to meet the minimum lender guidelines.*

- *The Collateral inside the house protects the lender first, while the Collateral outside the house protects the borrower first.*

- *Collateral as an eligibility requirement deems it important that you have either some Collateral in the house, or some outside the house, for most financing considerations.*

- *The four C's help balance one another. Collateral can impact the strictness of Character and Capacity, and vice versa.*

- *Your Credit score is generally the number one barrier and threat to use and control of the wealth in your house.*

- *Credit scores as an eligibility requirement make it important that you show a history of both willingness and ability to make your payments in a timely manner.*

- *Identify theft or a dramatic financial loss could rapidly drop your score to a level that makes borrowing difficult or impossible.*

- *External threats over which you have little or no control can affect your Credit in a way that immediately blocks future access to your wealth in the house.*

Chapter 5

Return

Compound interest is "the greatest mathematical discovery of all time." -- Albert Einstein

When you borrow, the interest you pay is the lender's Return. When you invest, the interest (or future growth) the borrower pays is your Return. We can define Return as the interest or growth you receive on money you lend for another's use and control.

Whether you are paying off liabilities or making new investments, few mysteries related to financial wealth creation are more exciting than the power of compound interest.

Return can have a dramatic influence on the amount you need to invest to reach a future financial goal over a specific period of time. The chart below shows the significance of Return on even a small investment compounded over various numbers of years.

Rate of Return*	$100 Invested Monthly					
12%	$8,167	$23,004	$98,926	$349,496	$1,176,477	$3,905,834
10%	$7,744	$20,484	$75,937	$226,049	$632,408	$1,732,439
8%	$7,348	$18,295	$58,902	$149,036	$349,101	$793,173
6%	$6,977	$16,388	$46,204	$100,452	$199,149	$378,719
4%	$6,630	$14,725	$36,677	$69,405	$118,196	$190,936
2%	$6,305	$13,272	$29,480	$49,273	$73,444	$102,961
0%	$6,000	$12,000	$24,000	$36,000	$48,000	$60,000
Years Invested	**5**	**10**	**20**	**30**	**40**	**50**
						***assumes after tax growth**

A chart like this doesn't teach us how to save. It does communicate that saving a great deal of money is possible if we are disciplined. We may not have a great deal of control over the Return we earn, but we do control how much we save. Based on this simple chart, I believed that I could eventually become a millionaire by saving $100 per month over an extended period of time. The amount of time was relative to the Return of my investment. As shown in the table, investing $100 per month for 50 years with an 8% Return would yield nearly $800,000. With a 10% Return, it would yield more than $1.7 million.

Let's review the goals of Safety, Liquidity, and Return:

- *Safety is about making sure your wealth will still be there when you need it.*

- *Liquidity is about making sure your wealth will be accessible when you need it.*

- *Return is about making sure that your wealth earns interest, or grows for a future purpose. (Because of inflation, the future value of your money will not have the same buying power as it does today.)*

The Role of Return in Creating Wealth

Return plays a role in both wealth preservation and wealth creation. If you had deposited $1,000 cash into a safe deposit box 30 years ago, it would only buy $160 worth of goods and services today. Due to inflation, a loaf of bread doesn't cost a nickel any more. In other words, the value of your money is relative to its ability to maintain its buying power over time.

- *Return must keep pace with inflation to preserve its ability to buy the same goods or services in the future.*

- *Return increases your wealth only to the extent that the Return you earn exceeds the rate of inflation.*

Consider a couple that purchased a house 15 years ago for $245,000. The house is worth $450,000. The value of the house increased by an average of 4% annually during this time. While the house increased their wealth, the wealth in their house is different from other types of investments.

In today's dollars, a house that sold for $245,000 15 years ago would now cost $364,000 based on inflation alone. That means in today's dollars the house has increased by only $86,000 ($450,000 minus $364,000), a 2.67% net Return. If they sold the house for $450,000, they'd receive $450,000 - $245,000, which is $205,000 of real money at closing. The catch - the $205,000 in today's money would spend like $86,000 would have spent 15 years ago. If they buy the same size house now, most of their gain gets lost in the new house. If they buy a smaller house, or decide to rent, they'd experience a more direct impact from their Return over time.

The Role of Return and Time

A 65-year-old couple might plan to live in their house for 30 more years. A 30-year-old couple buying their first house might expect to live in a house for 60 or more years. The combined impact of time and Return make our understanding of the concept of Return crucial to building future wealth.

The sooner you start investing, the greater the power of compounding interest. Refinancing every chance you get, and allowing that savings to work for you is critical when you combine it with the time value of money. Imagine you could refinance now to save $261 per month, or $3,132 per year. When you conisder a historical average Return of 8% over extended periods of time, I find no better illustration of compounding than this one. We'll use a 40 year time frame.

If you save the $3,132 annually for 8 years, and then stopped saving forever, your savings would grow to $422,289 over 40 years at an 8% after tax Return. Your total investment over the 8 years would have only been $25,056. If you subtract the $422,289 in future growth from the investment of $25,056, your net worth would have increased by $397,233.

What if I waited to the next opportunity to refinance 8 years later? If you save the $3,132 annually for the remaining 32 years, your savings would grow to $453,985 at an 8% after tax Return. Your total investment over those 32 years would be $100,224. If you subtract the $453,985 from the investment of $100,224, your net worth would have increased by $353,761 at age 65.

If you compare the future net worth of $397,233 versus $353,761, you realized a positive impact of $43,472 by starting early. The table on the following pages illustrates this in more detail. If you invested your savings for 32 total years in each scenario, but started 8 years earlier, your net worth would have increased to $740,071.

Study the following two illustrations, and consider the importance of acting now. What's happened up to this point is irrelevant. Foregiveness is giving up all hope of a better past. What action can you take now that might allow you to increase your cash flow to let compounding work toward your brighter future. You can't control the 8% Return, but you can control your behaviors that increase the likelihood of financial success.

Cost of Waiting 8 Years to Refinance

Age	Savings	Value Year End	Savings	Value Year End
25	$3,132	$3,383	8 Years	
26	$3,132	$7,036		
27	$3,132	$10,981		
28	$3,132	$15,242		
29	$3,132	$19,844		
30	$3,132	$24,814		
31	$3,132	$30,182		
32	$3,132	$35,979		
33		$38,857	$3,132	$3,383
34		$41,966	$3,132	$7,036
35		$45,323	$3,132	$10,981
36		$48,949	$3,132	$15,242
37		$52,865	$3,132	$19,844
38		$57,094	$3,132	$24,814
39		$61,662	$3,132	$30,182
40		$66,595	$3,132	$35,979
41		$71,922	$3,132	$42,240
42		$77,676	$3,132	$49,002
43		$83,890	$3,132	$56,304
44		$90,601	$3,132	$64,191
45		$97,849	$3,132	$72,709
46		$105,677	$3,132	$81,908
47		$114,132	$3,132	$91,844
48		$123,262	$3,132	$102,574
49		$133,123	$3,132	$114,162
50		$143,773	$3,132	$126,678
51		$155,275	$3,132	$140,194
52		$167,697	$3,132	$154,793
53		$181,112	$3,132	$170,559
54		$195,601	$3,132	$187,586
55		$211,250	$3,132	$205,975
56		$228,150	$3,132	$225,836
57		$246,402	$3,132	$247,285
58		$266,114	$3,132	$270,451
59		$287,403	$3,132	$295,469
60		$310,395	$3,132	$322,489
61		$335,227	$3,132	$351,671
62		$362,045	$3,132	$383,187
63		$391,008	$3,132	$417,225
64		$422,289	$3,132	$453,985
65	**$25,056**	**$422,289**	**$100,224**	**$453,985**
	Net Worth + $397,233		**Net Worth + $353,761**	

assumes 8% after tax annual growth rate

Cost of Waiting 8 Years to Refinance

Age	Savings	Value Year End	Savings	Value Year End
25	$3,132	$3,383	8 Years	
26	$3,132	$7,036		
27	$3,132	$10,981		
28	$3,132	$15,242		
29	$3,132	$19,844		
30	$3,132	$24,814		
31	$3,132	$30,182		
32	$3,132	$35,979		
33	$3,132	$42,240	$3,132	$3,383
34	$3,132	$49,002	$3,132	$7,036
35	$3,132	$56,304	$3,132	$10,981
36	$3,132	$64,191	$3,132	$15,242
37	$3,132	$72,709	$3,132	$19,844
38	$3,132	$81,908	$3,132	$24,814
39	$3,132	$91,844	$3,132	$30,182
40	$3,132	$102,574	$3,132	$35,979
41	$3,132	$114,162	$3,132	$42,240
42	$3,132	$126,678	$3,132	$49,002
43	$3,132	$140,194	$3,132	$56,304
44	$3,132	$154,793	$3,132	$64,191
45	$3,132	$170,559	$3,132	$72,709
46	$3,132	$187,586	$3,132	$81,908
47	$3,132	$205,975	$3,132	$91,844
48	$3,132	$225,836	$3,132	$102,574
49	$3,132	$247,285	$3,132	$114,162
50	$3,132	$270,451	$3,132	$126,678
51	$3,132	$295,469	$3,132	$140,194
52	$3,132	$322,489	$3,132	$154,793
53	$3,132	$351,671	$3,132	$170,559
54	$3,132	$383,187	$3,132	$187,586
55	$3,132	$417,225	$3,132	$205,975
56	$3,132	$453,985	$3,132	$225,836
57	8 Years	$490,304	$3,132	$247,285
58		$529,529	$3,132	$270,451
59		$571,891	$3,132	$295,469
60		$617,642	$3,132	$322,489
61		$667,053	$3,132	$351,671
62		$720,418	$3,132	$383,187
63		$778,051	$3,132	$417,225
64		$840,295	$3,132	$453,985
65	**$100,224**	**$840,295**	**$100,224**	**$453,985**
	Net Worth + $740,071		**Net Worth + $353,761**	

assumes 8% after tax annual growth rate

Calculating Return on Wealth in the House

Do you know the actual Return on the wealth you have invested in your house? Many people believe the equity in their house grows at the rate that their house appreciates.

It can be hard to understand how a house investment performs in comparison with other investments. The house value can go up or down, but that's true with most investments. The house has tax implications, but again that is true of most investments. The house could have a mortgage, and that's often where things get confusing. It's clear that your house has a major impact on your net worth, but it's not clear exactly how this occurs.

Let's focus first on the house. The house value can only go up or down through appreciation or depreciation. House value is a function of what the market will pay for your house, and because these changes aren't on your balance sheet, ongoing fluctuations in the value of your house will increase or decrease your net worth.

This is important to understand. Imagine that you own a house that is currently worth $200,000. Regardless of whether you have a $200,000 mortgage or no mortgage, if the house value increases 2%, you will have a house worth $204,000. Your net worth will therefore increase by $4,000. This has nothing to do with whether or not you have a mortgage.

One Year Appreciation of 2% = $4,000			
Assets		**Liabilities**	
Checking	$10,000	Mortgage	$160,000
Savings	$15,000	Auto Loans	$35,000
Investments	$175,000	Credit Cards	$5,000
House	**$204,000**		
Total	**$404,000**	**Total**	**$200,000**
Net Worth Increases from $200,000 to $204,000			

- *Net worth can only increase or decrease relative to market appreciation or depreciation of the house value.*
- *Technically, you must subtract inflation from appreciation or depreciation to understand the real impact on net worth.*
- *This is something over which you have very little control.*

If you have a mortgage, you can choose to make principal prepayments to repay that mortgage. Making principal payments will decrease your mortgage balance liability, and it will decrease your assets, but this has no impact on net worth today.

If you own a house that is currently worth $200,000, and you have a $200,000 mortgage, what if you choose to repay $8,000 of that mortgage? The mortgage would decrease to $192,000. This has no increase in the value of the house, and does not increase your net worth. You had to spend $8,000 from your checking account to increase your house equity by an equivalent amount. The $8,000 is your money that you would be moving from your pocket to the lender's pocket. Your benefit translates into reduced liabilities.

Mortgage Prepayment of $8,000			
Assets		**Liabilities**	
Checking	**$2,000**	Mortgage	**$152,000**
Savings	$15,000	Auto Loans	$35,000
Investments	$175,000	Credit Cards	$5,000
House	$200,000		
Total	**$392,000**	**Total**	**$192,000**
Net Worth Stays at $200,000			

- *Net equity through principal payments or principal withdrawals has no immediate impact on net worth.*

- *This is something over which you have a great deal of control.*

Net worth related to house ownership:

- *Increases only through appreciation (relative to inflation).*
- *Decreases only through depreciation (relative to inflation).*

Net equity in the house can increase in only two ways:

- *Through appreciation.*
- *Through down payment and principal repayment.*

Net equity in the house can decrease in only two ways:

- *Through depreciation.*
- *Through a withdrawal of principal. For example, a cash out mortgage that increased the loan balance.*

The important distinction is that appreciation and depreciation affect your net worth, while principal payments and withdrawals are balance sheet neutral – they have no impact on your net wealth when you make them.

That said, how do we calculate the Return on wealth in your house?

Example 1

Imagine that John and Mary Smith purchase a $200,000 house with a $40,000 investment using a $160,000, 30-year mortgage fixed at 6%. Their monthly payment is $960 (rounding up from $959.28).

Let's also assume that the house appreciates 2% in value each year (compounded annually). After 30 years, the house will be worth $364,242. The Smiths' net worth will increase by $164,242 through market appreciation of their house (not adjusted for inflation).

Initial Investment: $40,000				
Purchase Price: $200,000 **Mortgage: $160,000**		**Interest Rate: 6% (30-year amort.)** **Appreciation: 2% (annual)**		
	Day 1	**5 Years**	**15 Years**	**30 Years**
House Value	$200,000	$221,016	$269,904	$364,241
House Mortgage	$160,000	$148,887	$113,678	$0
House Equity	$40,000	$93,589	$245,630	$364,241
House Value	$+0	+$21,016	+$69,904	+$164,241
Net Worth	$+0	+$21,016	+$69,904	+$164,241

The Smiths' 30-year fixed mortgage required monthly payments of $960 during the term of the mortgage. At the end of the 30-year term, the mortgage will have a balance of $0. The initial investment of $40,000 and the principal repayment of $160,000 will increase the net equity in the house, but it will have no impact on their net worth. The $200,000 in principal was money they relocated from one asset to another asset.

One might assume that the $40,000 down payment grew to $364,241 over the 30 years. This is why Return on the house investment is more difficult to understand than most other investments. In reality, the Return on the house has nothing to do with the amount invested. The future wealth of $364,241 consists of $40,000 (the initial principal investment), plus $160,000 (the principal repaid over and above the mortgage interest paid), plus $164,241 (appreciation).

Any change in principal is a movement of wealth on your balance sheet. It's like moving money from your front pocket to your back pocket; the location changes but the amount of money you have does not.

Any change in house value increases or decreases your balance sheet. House appreciation or depreciation increases or decreases your actual net worth. Let's consider an alternative scenario.

Example 2

What happens if the appreciation is 0%?

Again, imagine that the Smiths are buying a $200,000 house with a $40,000 down payment and taking out a $160,000 mortgage for 30 years at a 6% fixed rate. Again, their monthly payments will be $960. Imagine an average annual appreciation of 0% over the entire 30-year period.

After 30 years with no appreciation, the house will still be worth $200,000. Therefore, the Smiths will gain no new wealth creation from their house. Their net equity will change over time as they repay principal, but their net worth will remain the same.

Initial Investment: $40,000				
Purchase Price: $200,000 Mortgage: $160,000		Interest Rate: 6% (30-year amort.) Appreciation: 0% (annual)		
	Day 1	**5 Years**	**15 Years**	**30 Years**
House Value	$200,000	$200,000	$200,000	$200,000
House Mortgage	$160,000	$148,887	$113,678	$0
House Equity	$40,000	$51,113	$86,332	$200,000
House Value	$+0	$+0	$+0	$+0
Net Worth	$+0	$+0	$+0	$+0

The Smiths' 30-year fixed mortgage requires monthly payments of $960 during the term of the mortgage. At the end of the 30-year term the mortgage will have a balance of $0. The initial investment of $40,000 and the repayment of the $160,000 increase the net equity in the house, but this has no impact on their net worth. Again, the $200,000 here is money they relocated from one asset (their check account) to another asset (their house).

We imagine that the $40,000 initially invested grows to $200,000 in 30 years. However, the monthly payments of $160,000 are paid by you to reduce your balance, and the interest is paid by you to the bank, no new wealth is created when you pay yourself with your own money.

Example 3

What would happen to the house investment if there were no appreciation and no repayment of principal?

This time, imagine the Smiths are buying a $200,000 house with a $40,000 down payment and borrowing $160,000 with a 6% fixed "interest-only" (IO) 30-year mortgage. Their payment will be $800 per month. With an IO mortgage, 100% of the monthly payments are for interest; there is no reduction of principal.

In 30 years, the house will still be worth $200,000. Therefore, the Smiths will gain no new wealth from owning their house. Their net equity will also remain unchanged, as no additional principal payments are made to reduce the house mortgage.

Initial Investment: $40,000				
Purchase Price: $200,000 **Mortgage: $160,000**		**Interest Rate: 6% (30-year IO)** **Appreciation: 0% (annual)**		
	Day 1	**5 Years**	**15 Years**	**30 Years**
House Value	$200,000	$200,000	$200,000	$200,000
House Mortgage	$160,000	$160,000	$160,000	$160,000
House Equity	$40,000	$40,000	$40,000	$40,000
House Value	$+0	$+0	$+0	$+0
Net Worth	$+0	$+0	$+0	$+0

The original investment is $40,000. If we subtract the value of the house in 30 years ($200,000) from the mortgage balance in 30 years ($160,000), we see that total wealth in the house is $40,000. The $40,000 in initial principal invested by the house buyer remains $40,000 after 30 years. Without appreciation, there is no positive impact on net worth. Without principal repayment, there is no increase in net equity in the house.

If you invest $40,000 and the investment is still worth $40,000 after 30 years, your investment has earned a 0% Return. It has had no growth. Thus, the ability of your house to influence your net worth boils down to whether or not the house's value appreciates or depreciates over time. The money you have inside the house doesn't earn a specific Return, but it does impact your interest, and that we'll discuss in the next chapter.

Example 4

Imagine the Smiths are buying a $200,000 house and have chosen to leave their $40,000 invested elsewhere. They borrow $200,000 for 30 years at a 6% fixed rate. Their payment will be $1,200 per month (rounded up from $1,199.10) . Let's also assume that the house will appreciate at 2% annually for 30 years.

Initial Investment: $0				
Purchase Price: $200,000 **Mortgage: $200,000**		**Interest Rate: 6% (30-year amort.)** **Appreciation: 2% (annual)**		
	Day 1	**5 Years**	**15 Years**	**30 Years**
House Value	$200,000	$221,016	$269,904	$364,241
House Mortgage	$200,000	$186,109	$142,098	$0
House Equity	$0	$34,907	$127,806	$364,241
House Value	$+0	+$34,907	+$127,806	+$364,241
Net Worth	$+0	+$34,907	+$127,806	+$364,241

Where $0 is invested to purchase a $200,000 house, the future wealth of $364,241 consists of $200,000 (the principal repaid over and above the mortgage interest paid), plus $164,241 (the appreciation of the value of the house). The impact to net worth from the house appreciation is the same from a net equity standpoint.

That said, did you find yourself wondering what was missing in the last few examples. Did you think we were ignoring the interest impact? In Example 1, the Smiths borrow $160,000. In Example 4, they borrow $200,000. In both cases, their net equity in the house after 30 years would be $364,241. If there were nothing missing here, there would be no reason ever to locate money in a house!

In fact, it's not just about interest. There are <u>four</u> missing ingredients.

Cash Flow & Interest

The first missing ingredient is cash flow. Borrowing $160,000 at 6% would result in monthly payments of $960, whereas borrowing $200,000 at 6% required monthly payments of $1,200. That's a difference of $240 per month over the term of 30 years. The decision to invest money inside the house, or not, will impact cash flow each month, and that impacts the interest charges on the outstanding balance of the loan.

Tax Savings

A second missing ingredient is tax savings. If the Smiths are in a 30% marginal tax bracket, a $160,000 mortgage would increase their itemized tax deductions, and reduce their net monthly cost by an average of $154 per month. A $200,000 mortgage would increase their itemized tax deductions further, and reduce their net monthly cost by an average of $193 per month. The $193 (minus) $154 = $39 in higher tax savings.

Borrowing $200,000 instead of $160,000 increases the tax savings by $39 per month. Subtracting the $39 tax savings from the $240 higher payment yields $201 as the average net after-tax increase in cash flow.

Use and Control of Down Payment

The third missing ingredient is the $40,000 down payment. Remember, if the Smiths invest $40,000 and borrow the remaining $160,000, they lose the use and control of the $40,000 for 30 years. If they borrow $200,000, they are paying higher interest in the form of net after-tax cash flow of $201 per month, but they retain the use and control of the $40,000. It starts to get confusing.

Impact of the Missing Ingredients			
Loan Amount	**Payment**	**Avg. Tax Savings**	**Available Cash**
$160,000	$960	$154	$0
$200,000	$1,200	$193	$40,000
Difference	**$240**	**$39**	**$40,000**
	$39 per month		**$40,000**
	$201 per month = $40,000 cash		

What is the cost of retaining use and control of the $40,000? Their after-tax cost was an average of $201 per month. The degree to which this is a positive or negative to the Smith's net worth, is the degree to which the $40,000 earns more or less than $201 per month in interest or future growth.

Inflation

The fourth missing ingredient is inflation. In our example where we show house appreciation, we used 2%. If inflation averaged 2% over the 30 years of house ownership, then the net impact to net worth would be $0. If the house appreciated at 4%, and inflation averaged 3%, then the true appreciation rate of the house relative to net worth would only be 1%.

If net worth related to the house only grows through relative property appreciation, and wealth in the house has no bearing on appreciation, and a large chunk of property appreciation is lost to inflation, then how do we understand the benefits of having our money located inside or outside the house? How do we maximize our long term wealth through owning real estate? How do the missing ingredients of cash flow, taxes and use and control of the down payment impact our decision as to the location of our wealth? What are the real costs, risks, and concerns of earning this higher Return? This brings us to the concept of EPR™.

Summary of Key Learnings

- Time, Amount and Return are three key factors that affect wealth accumulation.

- In choosing an investment product to transport wealth to a future Amount over a given period of time, the Return is as important as Safety and Liquidity.

- Return can have a major influence on small amounts of wealth over a long period of Time.

- Starting early can do a lot to help boost growth on the wealth you aim to have for your future.

- It's never too soon to start managing your wealth inside or outside the house.

- Change in wealth in the house is an external function of appreciation or depreciation, and an internal function of principal payments or principal withdrawals.

- Without appreciation or principal repayment, the wealth inside the house cannot grow. Only appreciation will increase net worth.

- The ability to deduct interest payments on your tax return helps reduce the cost of a mortgage payment.

- Wealth not invested in the house can be invested elsewhere.

- Wealth inside the house reduces monthly mortgage interest payments.

- *Wealth outside the house increases monthly mortgage interest payments.*

Chapter 6

EPR™

"It is not from the benevolence of the butcher, or the baker, that we expect our dinner, but from their regard to their own self interest." -- *Adam Smith*

There are two primary ways owning a house will influence your net worth over your life time. The first is the appreciation or depreciation of the house itself, over which you have very little control, and the second is the approach you take to borrowing, over which you have a great deal of control.

One of the fundamental decisions of borrowing relates to whether to locate wealth inside or outside the house. The initial decision has no immediate impact on net worth, but the long term decision could have a tremendous impact on your future wealth. Wealth located inside the house saves you interest at the current net after tax cost of borrowing. Wealth outside the house earns interest or grows at some net after tax return on the investment. Ultimately, the decision to pay down principal on your mortgage or take cash out can be driven by short term cash flow needs, or by a longer term desire to maximize wealth. It might also be driven by emotional needs around the 'home'.

How can you manage the principal in your house to maximize wealth creation? We must examine the cost of wealth that is located either inside or outside the house. We must also explore two associated concepts, which we'll call Market Risk and Discipline Risk. Understanding these concepts will help you answer the following questions:

- *Should I pay off my house using bi-weekly loan payments instead of monthly payments?*

- *Should I convert from a 30-year to a 15-Year fixed mortgage?*

- *Should I use my inheritance to prepay all or a portion of my mortgage?*

- *If I own a house with no mortgage, should I take out a mortgage on the house and invest the money elsewhere?*

- *Should I pay cash for a house?*

- *Should we use house equity to help pay for our children's education?*

- *When buying a new car, is it better to use house equity, pay cash, or use dealer financing?*

All of these questions involve decisions about locating wealth inside or outside your house. To help you make those decisions, I offer a simple concept called EPR™, or Effective Percentage Rate.

Understanding EPR™

The wealth in the house does not earn a specific Return based on appreciation or depreciation, as appreciation or depreciation operate independently of the wealth located in the house, as we discussed in the last chapter. However, wealth in the house reduces current borrowing needs, and as such, it reduces lender interest charges. This is where EPR™ comes into play. EPR™ is the net cost of interest based on the location of the money. Remember it's all about location, location, location.

If you borrow money on a credit card at a 12% annual rate of interest, the credit card company will earn a 12% Return. You are paying the credit card lender 12% interest in exchange for the use of their money. The EPR™ for using credit card debt is 12%.

When you borrow money using the house as collateral, the interest you pay may be tax-deductible. When you borrow money against the value of your house at 6%, the lender will earn a 6% Return. If you are in a 30% federal and state tax bracket, and your interest is tax-deductible, then the government will subsidize 30% of your interest burden. Thus, the net amount of interest you pay is reduced by 30% of the 6%. Since 30% of 6% is 1.8%, your actual cost of borrowing is 6% minus 1.8%, or 4.2%. In effect, paying 6% interest costs you only 4.2% on an after tax basis. The government provides these tax benefits to encourage house ownership.

EPR™ of Borrowing				
	Nominal Rate	**Tax Bracket**	**Tax-Favored**	**EPR™**
Credit Card	10%	30%	No	10%
Auto Loan	8%	30%	No	8%
Mortgage	6%	30%	Yes	4.2%

Wealth located inside the house eliminates interest that you would pay the lender for the use and control of the lender's money. The interest you save can be measured through EPR™. If your EPR™ is 4.2% for your current mortgage, money you locate inside the house saves you the 4.2% in annual interest cost. In this way you can understand that while wealth in the house earns no direct Return based on the appreciation or depreciation of the house investment, it does have a Return based on your individual interest rate and tax situation. This also means that money that you locate outside the house carries a 4.2% cost if you could have used that money to repay your debt.

By using EPR™ as a guide, we can more readily identify a hidden cost that might have been otherwise difficult to see.

A Hidden-Cost Parable

Nineteenth-century French economist Frederic Bastiat published a parable that describes a shopkeeper whose window is broken by a young boy. The people sympathize with the man whose window was broken, but soon they start to suggest that the broken window makes work for the glazier, who will then buy bread, benefitting the baker, who will then buy shoes, benefitting the cobbler, and so on. Finally, the onlookers conclude that the boy was not guilty of vandalism; instead he was a public benefactor who created economic benefits for nearly everyone in town.

Such benefits to the town were an illusion, in the way that someone without a mortgage believes that they are significantly better off financially than someone with a mortgage. This may not be the case. We would ideally locate our wealth relative to the highest and best use. A decision based on many things, but one that includes EPR™. This allows us to create a simple, repeatable process for borrowing decisions. The concept of using EPR™ will make it easier to quickly determine the cost of locating our money inside or outside the house. This can be very helpful when you need to make complex decisions quickly related to your borrowing.

In Bastiat's parable, imagine that the shopkeeper spends $20 to repair the broken window. After the window is replaced, his net gain is the same window he had originally. If the window hadn't been broken, the $20 could have purchased bread and shoes, benefitting both the baker and shopkeeper, resulting in true economic benefit. Or, the shopkeeper could have invested the $20 to earn interest over the years to come. Therefore, the townspeople misunderstood the Hidden Cost of replacing the window.

In much the same way, many of us with a mortgage believe that the mortgage should be paid off before we start getting serious about saving.

However, that approach has some hidden costs. For one thing, it means losing time to allow investment earnings to compound.

What can the parable of the broken window teach us about the Hidden Cost involving wealth in the house?

Through The Fog

Is it possible for you to borrow at 6% and invest at 6% and still increase your wealth? The answer depends on your individual situation. If your net (after-tax) cost of borrowing is 6% and your net (after-tax) benefit of investing is 6%, then the benefit of borrowing is purely one of Safety and Liquidity – having wealth where you want it and available when you need it. If your net (after-tax) cost of borrowing is 4% and your net (after-tax) benefit of investing is 6%, then the benefit of borrowing should increase your net worth over time.

Imagine that you invest $1,000 each month over a 30-year period and earn a 6% average annual Return net after taxes. During the same 30-year period, you could have made additional contributions of $1,000 to prepay your 6% mortgage. In other words you could save 4.2% by prepaying when you could have earned 6% by investing. That lost benefit is a cost that often remains hidden.

Thus, putting the money into your investment instead of using it to prepay a mortgage could boost your earnings by 1.8% (6% minus 4.2% = 1.8%). A 1.8% difference compounded over 30 years can make a real difference in the amount of wealth you accumulate.

Wealth Growing Inside or Outside		
Amount Invested:	**$1,000 monthly**	**$1,000 monthly**
Return:	4.2%*	6%*
Term:	30 years	30 years
Growth:	$720,225	$1,007,309
		**assumes an after tax rate of return*

Calculating EPR™

Calculating your EPR™ is very simple, and it's a necessity for managing present and future decisions about the location of your wealth. Here's how to do it:

- *Step 1: List all of your liabilities on the following chart by Liability Name first. Then insert the interest rate you are paying into the appropriate column, put interest rates for your mortgage, equity loans or other debt you know to be deductible in the Tax Deductible column. Insert the interest rates of other liabilities under the Not Tax Deductible column. These may include credit card debt, a car loan, equity line if you trigger AMT, mortgage loans if you don't itemize, and other consumer loans. Leave the EPR™* column blank for now.

EPR™ Worksheet			
Not Tax Deductible	**Liability Name**	**Tax Deductible**	**EPR™**
	First Mortgage	6.00	4.20%
8.00	Auto Loan		
Insert Your Liabilities Here			

Step 2. Use the following chart to estimate your marginal federal tax bracket based on your gross income. Then, add your state tax rate. The total is your state and federal marginal tax bracket. When you save money

from itemized deductions, it comes off your highest tax bracket. If you are married filing jointly and have combined income of $100,000, you would be in a 25% federal bracket. If your state tax rate is 5%, then add together for a total of 30% as your marginal rate.

Annual Federal Income Tax Brackets				
Marginal Tax Rate	**Single**	**Married Filing Jointly**	**Married Filing Separately**	**Head of Household**
10%	$0 - $8,700	$0 - $17,400	$0 - $8,700	$0 - $12,400
15%	$8,701 - $35,350	$17,401 - $70,700	$8,701 - $35,350	$12,401 - $47,350
25%	$35,351 - $85,650	$70,701 - $142,700	$35,351 - $71,350	$47,351 - $122,300
28%	$85,651 - $178,650	$142,701 - $217,450	$71,351 - $108,725	$122,301 - $198,050
33%	$178,651 - $388,350	$217,451 - $388,350	$108,726 - $194,175	$198,051 - $388,350
35%	over $388,350	over $388,350	over $194,175	over $388,350

**or Qualified Widow(er)*

- *Step 3. Go back to your EPR™ chart. Apply all of your listings in the Tax Deductible column to the following EPR™ formula:*

1. Remove the percentage sign. If your mortgage interest rate is 6.00%, use 6.00.
2. Multiply this number by your state and federal marginal tax bracket. For example, if your marginal tax bracket is 30% this year and your interest rate is 6.00%, then multiply 6.00 X .30 = 1.80. The total is your tax savings. Your tax savings reduces your cost of borrowing.
3. Take the tax savings (1.80 in the example), and subtract from your step 1 total (6.00 in the sample). The total is your EPR™ (your estimated cost of borrowing). In this sample, 6.00 – 1.80 = 4.20, so 4.20% is your EPR™.

4. In the EPR™ column of the chart, write the EPR™ for each item in the left-hand column.

By listing your liabilities and calculating their EPR™, you can better understand EPR™ opportunities.

What if you realize that you are carrying a credit card balance at 12%, and prepaying your mortgage of 6%, but the mortgage really costs you 4.2%? You could increase your Return by 7.8% by paying your credit card first.

What if your company matches your 401(k) contribution by 25%? Imagine that you are contributing $300 each month to the 401(k) and prepaying your mortgage by an extra $200 per month. You have one foot on the gas, and one foot on the brake. Prepaying your mortgage saves you 4.2%, but an investment in your 401(k) earns you 25% from your employer plus the investment Return on the account. You would be better off contributing the extra $200 per month to the 401(k) instead of prepaying the mortgage.

- *The EPR™ of money borrowed for a house is reduced by the tax deductible portion of the interest paid.*

- *The EPR™ of money borrowed for credit cards, auto loans, and personal loans is not reduced by the borrower's tax bracket. Interest on consumer loans is not tax-deductible.*

What if you have a house with no mortgage? The calculation is the same. You would use the current market interest rate for a mortgage. If you could gain use and control of wealth related to your house by borrowing at 6.00% and you are in a 30% tax bracket, then

Interest Savings With No Mortgage
6.00 X .30 = 1.80
6.00 - 1.80 = 4.20 EPR™

Having your house paid off saves you interest of 4.2% based on current market rates. You are saving interest of 4.2% that you would pay to a lender if you had a mortgage. If your alternative is an investment with an after-tax Return of 6%, then your decision to locate wealth in the house has a Hidden Cost of 1.8%.

When to Invest House Wealth

Sometimes it makes sense to locate wealth outside the house for Safety and Liquidity reasons. If the primary reason to relocate wealth is for increased Return, you would have to identify investments that you expect would earn a higher Return than your cost of borrowing.

The Safety, Liquidity, and Return of different investments can vary considerably. If you are contemplating a relocation of wealth, consider working with a financial advisor to assess the suitability of investments that provide the right mix of Safety, Liquidity and Return. Also, when analyzing a relocation of wealth outside the house, consider the importance of Market Risk and Discipline Risk on your final decision.

Market Risk

Market Risk is the risk that your Return on money moved outside the house could earn less than your net cost of borrowing. If your net cost of borrowing is 4.2%, then principal located outside the house must earn at least 4.2% to maintain your relative net worth. Given that 4.2% inside the house is essentially a guaranteed Return, you should generally expect to earn a higher rate on investments outside the house to compensate for the higher Market Risk.

Wealth outside the house can be lost through market conditions, changing interest rates, or poor investment decisions. Any money invested outside the house will be exposed to some Market Risk in order to increase its potential Safety, Liquidity and Return.

- *Wealth outside the house must earn a Return to offset the cost of having that money outside the house.*

- *Wealth outside the house will have some Market Risk that is different from wealth left inside the house.*

Discipline Risk

Discipline Risk is the risk that the ease with which you may access your wealth could increase your chances of spending money that you might otherwise not have spent. With increased Liquidity comes increased use and control. If you lack financial self-discipline and spend money you had intended to save, you are undermining your choice to move principal outside the house to build greater wealth. The less self-discipline you have with your money, the more you need to consider Discipline Risk as a factor in your wealth-building strategy.

An advisor can be of great service in helping to minimize Discipline Risk. If you think you would be more likely to spend money if you move it outside the house, you should either leave the money inside the house or consider adopting an automated savings system or direct payroll savings deduction. Instead of a monthly savings plan, a lump sum could be made. Alternatively, you could establish an agreement with your financial advisor stipulating that he or she will "approve" any spending from an account that you've set up solely to pay off your house.

- *If you spend the money that would otherwise be part of your future house wealth, you would have been better off leaving that money inside the house.*

Summary of Key Learnings

- *EPR™, or Effective Percentage Rate, can be used to help solve many difficult questions you may have about your mortgage.*

- *The EPR™ of money borrowed for a house is reduced by the borrower's tax bracket. It can be tax-favorable.*

- *The EPR™ of money borrowed for credit cards, auto loans, and personal loans is not reduced by the borrower's tax bracket. It is not tax-favorable.*

- *The EPR™ of money you invest in mutual funds, stocks, bonds, and certain other investments might or might not be tax-favorable.*

- *If the internal and external EPR™ are the same, the decision related to location revolves around your preferences for Safety or Liquidity.*

- If money kept outside the house is spent rather than invested, it won't generate future wealth.

Chapter 7

Taxes

"This [preparing my tax return] is too difficult for a mathematician. It takes a philosopher." -- Albert Einstein

Taxes play an important role in determining the actual cost, or EPR™, of borrowing. Taxes can also have a major impact on the amount you receive when selling your house. It is important to pay close attention to tax considerations any time you sell a house, buy a house, or refinance your house. Future changes in the tax laws might reduce certain tax benefits now available, so it can be very helpful to discuss your specific options with a tax advisor.

If you deduct mortgage interest on your income tax return, the tax savings comes off your highest applicable state and federal tax bracket. If, for example, you are in a 30% bracket for federal and state taxes, any savings generated through interest tax deductions on your house will be applied at the 30% level starting with the first dollar of savings.

Selling a House: Capital Gains

When you sell a house, your main tax consideration is the impact of capital gains taxes. Under current Internal Revenue Code Section 121 you can sell your house every 2 years and keep up to $250,000 in profits tax free. If you and your spouse file jointly and meet the requirements, you can keep up to $500,000 in profits tax free. You should consult a tax advisor for your specific situation, or research at www.irs.gov.

Many property owners manage to supplement their income by moving into a house and fixing it up while living there for two or more years, then selling and enjoying the tax-free gains. The tax impact is important when you sell. If you sell a house and also plan to buy a new house, you need to consider the tax impact of your purchase. Any gain up to $500,000 can be repositioned into other investments tax free if not put directly back into the house.

If you move out of your primary residence and convert it to a rental you still get the full benefits of Section 121 if you sell the house within 2 years of your conversion. However, after December, 2008 the tax law changed if you make a former rental property your new primary. It states that if you transition the house from use as a rental to use as a primary residence, you must prorate the capital gains exemption for purpose of calculating capital gains. Example: You have a beach house that you've rented for 5 years, and you move into that beach house in retirement. You live there for 5 years and sell the property. At the time of sale your profit is $200,000. Because it was a rental first, you would have to prorate the gains - 5 years of primary / 10 years of total = 50%. In this example, 50% of the $200,000 would be tax free, and 50% of the $200,000 would be considered as capital gains for tax purposes.

Buying a House: Interest Deductions

If you have profits from the sale of a house and you need to borrow additional money to buy a new house, the amount you borrow depends partly on how much you choose to reinvest from the sale of the prior house into the purchase of the new house. If you are buying a $200,000 house and you have $80,000 in tax-free gains from the sale of your previous house, you have some new opportunities. As discussed in the previous chapter, EPR™ might play a role in determining where you locate your wealth. The tax consequences of your decision may be another crucial factor.

If you are borrowing to buy a house, you pay interest to the lender. If you pay cash for a house, you save the interest you would have paid to the lender, but you lose the interest or return you might have earned by investing the money elsewhere. The tax deductibility of your mortgage interest reduces your net cost of borrowing, but only if the mortgage interest is indeed tax-deductible.

Under current Internal Revenue Code Section 163(h)(3), the interest paid on a mortgage is tax-deductible if it is incurred to acquire, construct, or substantially improve any qualified residence. You are allowed one primary and one secondary residence for purposes of interest deductibility if the mortgage is secured by that residence, and if it does not exceed the value of the residence. In other words, if you borrow money to buy, build, or improve a house and your loan uses the house as collateral, then the interest on your loan is tax-deductible as long as you don't borrow more than the value of the house. The loan principal on which interest is deductible may not exceed a combined $1 million (if you are married filing jointly, a single filer or a head of household filer) or $500,000 if you are married filing separately.

In addition, borrowing that is not incurred to acquire, construct, or substantially improve any qualified residence is deductible as long as the combined loans don't exceed the fair market value of the residence. However, the interest deductibility is capped at the principal amount of $100,000 (if you are married filing jointly, a single filer or a head of household filer) or $50,000 if married filing separately.

The maximum allowable borrowing for purpose of mortgage interest deductibility on IRS Form 1040 Schedule A is $1.1 million. This amount is based on a maximum of $1,000,000 for acquisition indebtedness, and a maximum of $100,000 of equity indebtedness on a single primary and a single secondary residence.

There are two catches to mortgage interest deductibility. First, there is a 3% deduction phase-out at higher Adjusted Gross Income (AGI) levels. This phase-out is not limited to mortgage interest. It is a flat phase-out of all itemized deductions based on income. It is capped at 80% of total itemized deductions. The second catch is the Alternative Minimum Tax.

Adjusted Gross Income Phase-Out

While there is a phase out of deductions for high income earners, there are no specific phase outs that solely targets mortgage interest deductibility.

In most states, it is impossible to phase-out all deductions for high income earners, because the higher income itself that triggers AGI phase-out actually produces additional itemized tax deductions (such as state income taxes) that push the maximum income threshold further out. You can generally assume that you'll experience a phase-out of all deductions (not specifically mortgage interest) if you make over the high income earner limit.

Alternative Minimum Tax (AMT)

An estimated 30 million tax returns could trigger the Alternative Minimum Tax (AMT) this year if the AMT patch isn't extended. AMT was designed to have everyone pay their fair share of taxes regardless of deductions and loopholes. Because AMT has not been adjusted for inflation, even though the regular tax brackets are, more and more taxpayers are triggering AMT with each passing year.

If you are subject to the AMT, then 100% of your acquisition indebtedness interest (borrowing of up to $1 million that was used to acquire, construct or improve) is fully deductible regardless of your income. In other words, the "phase-out" regarding your AGI is a non-issue if you pay the AMT. However, any equity indebtedness (borrowing not used to acquire, construct or improve) your house is not deductible. Additionally, any property taxes you pay are also not deductible if you are subject to the AMT.

Your tax professional should be able to determine whether or not you exceed the AGI phase-out limit or trigger AMT. When you calculate your EPR™ to figure out your cost of borrowing, consider whether either of these two provisions could reduce your tax deductibility.

- *If you are subject to AMT, your AMT tax rate is 26% or 28%, not the regular federal tax bracket used in the prior chapter table.*

Buying a House: Tax Impact of the Down Payment

A down payment cannot exceed 100% of the cost of a house. If you make a 100% down payment, there is no interest to deduct on your tax return. Any future first mortgage loan is only deductible if used to improve the house.

The minimum down payment you can make is 0%. If you make no down payment, and borrow 100% of the needed funds, you have the highest possible loan amount for interest deductibility. Because the loan will be used to acquire, construct, or improve the property, the interest you pay is tax-deductible up to the $1 million of principal debt.

In determining the size of a down payment, you should consider the impact of mortgage insurance, tax deductibility of the mortgage interest, and payment cash flow.

Any first mortgage loan amount that exceeds 80% will typically require either mortgage insurance or a higher interest rate on the mortgage. Mortgage insurance may not be deductible, a higher interest rate to lender finance the mortgage insurance is often a better financial move.

If you want to borrow more than 80% of the purchase price, consider borrowing 80% as a first mortgage and the remaining percentage as an equity line of credit or second mortgage. One exception is a special arrangement such as a pledged asset mortgage where you can borrow

100% of the loan amount without mortgage insurance.

Many buyers don't consider the impact of the down payment on mortgage interest deductibility. The amount of the mortgage that is deductible as acquisition indebtedness is the loan amount that was used to acquire, construct, or improve the property. If you purchase a new house for $400,000 and you borrow $200,000, then $200,000 is the amount used to acquire, construct or improve the property. That is the amount of the loan that is tax-deductible. If you purchase a new house for $400,000 and borrow $0, then $0 is tax deductible under acquisition indebtedness.

What if you purchase the house for $400,000 with cash, and a year later you decide to refinance the house and borrow $200,000 for your child's education? At this point the $200,000 is not being used to acquire, construct, or improve the house, so it would not be deductible as part of your acquisition indebtedness. You can deduct the interest on up to $100,000 borrowed for any for any purpose as part of your equity indebtedness (with the exception of Section 264 limitations on the purchase of life insurance and certain tax preferred products), so the interest on $100,000 of the $200,000 would be deductible as long as you were not subject to AMT.

This is an important consideration. Many unknowing buyers pay cash for convenience, then later on decide to borrow for another reason without realizing they've lost their acquisition indebtedness interest deductibility on that property.

- *You can, however, finance within 90 days of your purchase and still have the loan qualify as acquisition indebtedness up to the $1 million limit.*
- *If you wait 91 days or more, a mortgage loan that is used for investment or business purposes could be fully deductible on other tax return schedules with no limit on the amount borrowed.*

If having the maximum tax deductibility is important to you, then consider starting out with the highest possible loan available–up to 100% of the purchase price–to set the available mortgage deductibility at the highest possible level.

There are also several different ways you can pay your mortgage that will impact the tax deductibility over your loan term. These include: amortizing; interest-only; and negative amortizing.

Types of Payment

With an amortizing loan, you pay principal and interest each month. Thus, each month you are permanently reducing your interest deductibility by paying down your principal. If you were to borrow $200,000 at 6%, you'd pay back about $13,891 in principal after 5 years. That means your mortgage balance would be approximately $186,109. If you refinance the house with a cash-out loan back to the original $200,000, the $13,891 is not tax deductible under acquisition indebtedness unless the full $13,891 is being used to improve the house. The $13,891 would be deductible under the $100,000 equity indebtedness cap if you are not subject to AMT. Each year you pay down an amortizing loan, you are losing future deductibility.

If you pay your loan as an interest-only loan-say you borrow $200,000 with an interest-only loan at 6%–you are paying interest each month and you are not reducing your balance. In five years, your mortgage balance will be $200,000, and your potential mortgage interest deductibility will still be $200,000 of debt principal. An interest-only loan maintains the original interest deductibility that qualified as acquisition indebtedness, while amortizing loans reduce the mortgage interest deductibility with each principal payment.

If you pay your loan as a negative amortizing (a Reverse Mortgage) loan-say you borrow $200,000 with a negative amortization loan at 6%–you will pay interest each month, but that interest is added to your loan balance each month. Your loan balance in five years would be $269,770. Your acquisition indebtedness would remain at $200,000 of debt principal, and the additional $69,770 would be deductible under equity indebtedness as long as the total loan amount does not exceed the value of the house. The catch is that you don't get to write that interest off until you pay off the mortgage. That means the tax deductibility is there and available, but not realized until some point in the future when the debt is repaid.

Buying a House – Down Payment Impact on Payment

The more interest you are paying on a mortgage loan, the more you may be able to deduct, so a high loan balance can help to maximize tax deductibility. A high balance also means a high monthly payment. If you are comfortable with a larger loan and a higher payment, you may benefit by borrowing more and investing the funds outside the house, but if you don't earn a net return that is higher than your net cost of borrowing, you are losing ground.

If you have a monthly payment maximum and want to maximize the tax deductibility of the mortgage interest, you might borrow the maximum amount available based on your maximum payment, allowing the balance of the down payment to stay in an investment or savings account.

- *When selling a house, you want to consider advantages of a tax free gain by using "gain on sale" benefits of IRS Code Section 121.*
- *When buying a house, you want to consider the impact of taxes on interest rate deductibility based on IRS code Section 163.*

The time to make these decisions is at the time of purchase, or at least within 90 days of purchase. After 90 days have passed, your only future tax-advantaged access to the wealth inside the house is through cash-out refinancing or equity lines of credit, which limits you to $100,000 in mortgage interest deductibility unless that cash out is used for other tax deductible purposes.

Refinancing a House: Interest Rate Deductibility

If you access wealth in your house by refinancing, you generally have a choice of two possible loan types: (1) rate and term; and (2) cash out.

With a rate and term loan, the mortgage amount doesn't increase above the amount you currently owe, so the mortgage interest is fully deductible (subject to AGI and AMT considerations). If the loan is cash out, then the amount of principal upon which the interest is deductible will be subject to the amount of the current loan principal, plus additional improvements made to the house, plus up to $100,000 of equity indebtedness.

Let's say that over 10 years you pay a $300,000 mortgage down to $100,000. Recently you made $25,000 worth of additional house improvements. The house has increased in value to $500,000, and you would like to borrow $400,000. Using this formula, the $100,000 current principal balance + $25,000 in recent house improvements + $100,000 in equity indebtedness (if not subject to AMT) = $225,000. Of the $400,000 in new borrowing, technically only $225,000 of the amount borrowed would qualify for mortgage interest deductibility. I say "technically" because most people don't follow this rule and instead deduct all the interest on their form 1098. Should an audit occur, the taxpayer is often forced to pay the taxes with penalties.

I would advise anyone considering a cash house purchase to talk with a tax advisor before making a final decision. If you borrow, you can pay off the mortgage later. If you pay cash, you establish $0 as your acquisition indebtedness basis, and you'll be able to deduct no more than $100,000 (if not subject to AMT) should you later decide to take out a new mortgage loan for any purpose other than house improvements.

If you plan to refinance a house you already own, ask a tax professional to help you determine how much of the new mortgage will be deductible, and which schedule to utilize if you exceed the acquisition or equity indebtedness limits.

If you have a highly appreciated house, or one that is larger than you need, you could sell the house and potentially take a tax-free gain of up to $500,000. Then you could purchase another house and borrow up to 100% (if available) to maximize the interest deductibility by resetting the maximum loan available to you with the acquisition of a new house. Consider any closing costs and sales fees as a reduction of net benefits.

Grandfathering / Loan Fees

If you took out your loan before October 14, 1987, all interest is deductible per grandfathering provisions in the Tax Reform Act of 1986. This is only applicable if your acquisition or equity indebtedness was in excess of $1 million.

Late payment charges, prepayment penalties, and real estate taxes are usually deductible unless lost through AMT. In addition, points paid as prepaid interest are deductible over the life of the loan, while points paid to purchase a property may be written off in the transaction year. Interest on a house other than your primary or secondary house, such as an investment property, is deductible if the property is used for investment, business or other qualified purposes, and may be deducted on form 4952 subject to applicable limitations.

Mistakes to Avoid

Loans against the house that would normally be deductible will lose their tax deductibility if the money is used to purchase a single premium life insurance endowment or annuity contract, or for tax-exempt investments, like a tax-exempt municipal bond as per Section 264 of the IRS code.

If you pay cash for a house and then finance it more than 90 days after the purchase, your maximum interest rate deductibility is capped at the $100,000 equity indebtedness limit unless those additional amounts can be documented as a reinvestment into the house.

For debts to be included in the acquisition indebtedness as debts used to improve the property, the IRS recommends under IRS Notice 88-74 that the improvements must be made within 24 months of when the debt was incurred, AND no later than 90 days after the completion of the improvements.

If you finance your house privately by borrowing from an individual instead of a bank, the mortgage interest is only deductible if the lender records a note binding the house as collateral against the loan.

If you use an equity line of credit for a purchase, the interest will not be tax deductible if you are subject to AMT.

If you have a $1 million primary residence with no mortgage and you secure a $500,000 loan against that house to pay cash for a new secondary residence, only $100,000 of the $500,000 would be tax deductible as equity indebtedness.

IRS Monitoring

Each year, your mortgage lender must report the amount of interest you've paid on IRS Form 1098. The IRS has few systems in place to monitor this form and separate how much of the interest you are allowed to deduct on your tax return based on either acquisition or equity indebtedness.

This area has been considered one of the top audit watches for tax revenue recaptures and increases. In the future, it would be wise to make the tax nuances part of your planning process when you sell, buy or refinance a house. It's one more step toward Borrowing and Repaying Smart.

Summary of Key Learnings

- *Current law allows a taxpayer to deduct up to $1.1 million in tax-deductible interest as part of their Section 163 deductions.*
- *The higher your tax bracket, the more you can benefit from mortgage interest deductions, but you must itemize to receive a tax deduction (Schedule A) for the mortgage interest you've paid.*
- *If you pay principal and interest on a mortgage loan, the base Acquisition Indebtedness is decreasing each month, because the amount of principal you owe decreases.*
- *If you have an interest-only loan, the base Acquisition Indebtedness is level each month, because the mortgage balance is not decreasing.*
- *If you pay cash for a house, you are setting Acquisition Indebtedness to the lowest possible level. You are stuck with this level until you sell the house and purchase a new one.*

NOTES:

- *Write down things you might want to ask, or consider talking with your CPA about here:*

Chapter 8

Leverage

"Give me a lever long enough and a place to stand, and I will move the world." -- *Archimedes*

In physics, Leverage is the use of a lever (tool) to amplify force over a specific distance (or time). In finance, Leverage is the use of a small amount of money to control a larger amount of money. When allowing money to grow, time is very important. Leverage is like a time machine for money. It allows a smaller asset to control a larger asset, decreasing the amount of time it takes for the money to grow (or shrink) in value.

If you buy a house with cash, you employ no leverage. If you buy a house using a mortgage, you are using financial leverage that amplifies the Return on the investment. If you buy a $200,000 house with a $40,000 principal investment and a $160,000 mortgage, the $160,000 is the leverage you are using. By using this Leverage, your $40,000 investment can control a $200,000 asset. If the asset appreciates 2%, you gain 2% on the asset that you control (the $200,000 house) as opposed to the $40,000 invested.

The value of an asset will rise or fall based on the degree to which Leverage is utilized. A mechanical lever, properly positioned, can help you move a larger object with less effort. In financial leverage, an investor can control a larger asset in much the same way. In our example, the house owner gains use and control of a $200,000 asset (the house) with $40,000 cash (the investment). If $40,000 cash is invested in a stock, it controls $40,000 in stock. A stock investment of this type has no leverage, so a $1 loss is a $1 loss, and a $1 gain is a $1 gain. If you control a house worth $200,000 with a $40,000 investment, you have Leverage of 5 to 1. We can use a very simple formula to calculate leverage: asset controlled / investment made = degree of leverage.

Impact of Borrowing Leverage			
House Asset Value: $200,000	**2% Appreciation = $4,000**	**Future Value After 1 Year**	
Investment Amount [Down Payment %]	**Leverage Ratio**	**House Equity**	**Return Rate**
$0 [0%]	infinite	$4,000	infinite
$5,000 [2.5%]	40.00X	$9,000	80%
$10,000 [5%]	20.00X	$14,000	40%
$20,000 [10%]	10.00X	$24,000	20%
$40,000 [20%]	5.00X	$44,000	10%
$100,000 [50%]	2.00X	$104,000	4%
$200,000 [100%]	1.00X	$204,000	2%

$200,000 (house value) / $40,000 (cash investment) = 5:1, or 5X of leverage. That means every 1% movement in the value of the house creates a 5% movement in the investment.

$40,000 (stock value) / $40,000 (cash investment) = 1:1, or 1X of leverage. Every 1% movement in the value of the stock creates a 1% movement in that investment. If a margin account were used, the Leverage would impact the investment in much the same way.

The table on the left explains the impact of leverage based on different possible investment amounts used to control a $200,000 house, and the value after one year of house appreciation at 2%.

The 2% appreciation on the $200,000 house adds $4,000 in new wealth, offset by the interest expense. Based on the degree of leverage, we can see the impact on the original investment. The investment of 5%, or $10,000 invested, is worth $14,000 after one year of appreciation, which is 40% growth. The 2% appreciation had a 20X impact, such that the $4,000 in new equity was 40% growth on the original $10,000 investment. This works both ways. If the house were to decrease in value by 2%, it would be worth $196,000. If you had invested $10,000 in this house, you would have lost 40% of your investment based on a 2% decrease in value of the asset (the house).

Leverage, Return and the Rule of 72

Albert Einstein is credited with discovering the Rule of 72 when he was studying the concept of compound interest. The rule is simple. You divide the interest rate you expect to earn into the number 72. Doing this tells you how long it will take for your money to double in value. If you are earning 8% in an investment, divide 8% into 72 and you get 9 years. Your money invested at 8% would double every 9 years. The higher the return the faster the money doubles, and vice versa. That's how Leverage acts like a time machine for your money. Leverage can amplify the Return, reducing the time it would take for money to double in value.

Two Neighbors

What if two neighbors, John and Terry, each purchase their house with different investment amounts? John purchases a $200,000 house with a $100,000 mortgage? John controls a $200,000 asset (the house) with a $100,000 cash investment. The house appreciates 2%, and at the end of the first year, the house is worth $204,000. Using our formula for growth: $204,000 (current investment value) – $200,000 (original investment value) / $100,000 (cash used to control the asset) = 4% (growth rate on the cash used to control the asset).

John's neighbor, Terry, purchases a $200,000 house with a $180,000 mortgage. Terry controls a $200,000 asset (the house) with a $20,000 cash investment. The house appreciates 2%, and at the end of the first year, the house is worth $204,000. Using our formula for growth: $204,000 (current investment value) – $200,000 (original investment value) / $20,000 (cash used to control the asset) = 20% (growth rate on the cash used to control the asset). The 20% growth rate is 5 times the 4% growth rate earned by John because Terry used only $20,000 to control the $200,000 house.

Remember, the return on the house asset is a function of appreciation or depreciation, and has nothing to do with the wealth located in the house. The amount you invest in the house does impact the amount of Leverage that is used. The house value would have grown by 2% regardless of whether John had invested $20,000 or $100,000. The more wealth employed to control the house asset, the lower the degree of Leverage. The less wealth employed to control the house asset, the higher degree of Leverage.

Impact of Leverage and Appreciation on Return

House Asset Value: $200,000	**X**	**House Appreciation Rate:**		
		2%	**4%**	**6%**
Wealth Used to Control the House Asset	**Leverage Ratio**	**Effective Growth Rate:**		
$0	infinite	infinite	infinite	infinite
$5,000	40	80%	160%	240%
$10,000	20	40%	80%	120%
$20,000	10	20%	40%	60%
$40,000	5	10%	20%	30%
$100,000	2	4%	8%	12%
$200,000	1	2%	4%	6%

You can see above how slight moves in appreciation, combined with different degrees of Leverage, lead to wide variations in growth rates relative to the wealth used to control the asset.

In the U.S. economy, more private wealth has been created through real estate than through any other single investment. Americans' house wealth wasn't created through the investment of vast sums of money. Rather, it came from relatively small sums that worked over time with the powerful impact of both compound interest and Leverage. The result: new wealth based on "compound leverage."

At this point, you might jump to a conclusion that you should have as little equity in your house as possible to provide the highest possible real rate of Return through Leverage, but you also need to consider suitability based on the following: your risk tolerance; your time horizon; your EPR™; your need for liquidity; your goals for the real estate; and other considerations. For this reason it's important to look at the overall diversification of your assets in relation to all of your long-term goals.

Summary of Key Learnings

- *Leverage amplifies force. In the case of financial Leverage it increases or decreases the rate of growth to the degree it is used.*

- *The primary example of Leverage in real estate is the use of a small down payment to control a higher-value house. If you borrow, you are using Leverage. If you pay cash, there is no Leverage employed.*

- *When Leverage is employed, the appreciation is on the asset controlled. In the case of real estate, the house value appreciates; the asset used to control the house asset does not.*

- *Wealth created by real estate investing uses the power of compound interest, with the Return often amplified by Leverage.*

- *Compound Leverage is why real estate is such a great wealth creator in the U.S.* ▪

Chapter 9

Diversification

"Wide diversification is only required when investors do not understand what they are doing." -- *Warren Buffett*

Diversification in an investment portfolio offers the potential to earn the same target Return with less overall risk. It is one of the only "free lunches" available to the investor. If you have invested substantially in one particular asset or type of investment, you could reduce the risk by spreading your investments into investments of a similar Return that are of a different nature.

Putting all your eggs in one basket is risky, because unexpected losses can occur with any investment. Therefore, diversification plays an important role in reducing risk while building wealth.

House values fluctuate in response to local and national economic trends and other factors. The compounding of Time, Return, Leverage and related forces begs us to consider how much of our wealth should be allocated inside the house in comparison with other investment holdings. Viewing the house investment as an integral part of a well-diversified portfolio can help you achieve the highest possible return based on your individual tolerance for risk.

If you have $100,000 to invest, you might choose a combination of stocks, bonds, life insurance, mutual funds, cash, or other investments to spread out your risk. Most common investments fall into the broad-based categories of cash, bonds, and stocks. Let's look at three different scenarios for investing $100,000 based on different risk preferences within those three categories. First we'll compare an investment made in 1985 - 2015, and then we'll compare the growth of $100,000 over the last 30 years.

Aggressive		**Moderate**		**Conservative**	
Stocks	$100,000	Stocks	$60,000	Stocks	
Bonds		Bonds	$40,000	Bonds	$100,000
	$100,000		**$100,000**		**$100,000**
	Performance (1985 - 2015)*		Performance (1985 - 2015)*		Performance (1985 - 2015)*
Avg. Annual Return:	**11.86%**	**Avg. Annual Return:**	**8.70%**	**Avg. Annual Return:**	**6.88%**
Best Yr:	**54.20%**	**Best Yr:**	**36.70%**	**Best Yr:**	**32.60%**
Worst Yr:	**-43.10%**	**Worst Yr:**	**-26.60%**	**Worst Yr:**	**-8.10%**
$100,000 growth from 1985 - 2015**	**$3,448,527**		**$1,347,160**		**$783,112**

**Stocks based on S&P500 Vanguard Historical Index Performance*
*** Portfolio Visualizer Historical Growth Simulator*

Higher risk does not guarantee a higher Return, but you would only knowingly take higher risks if you believed there was an opportunity for higher Returns. In the above table, we can see that the best years and the worst years for Return were the farthest apart for the Aggressive investor, and closest together for the Conservative investor. Risk involves unpredictability. In the first chart, the Aggressive investor had a 4.98% higher average annual Return than the Conservative investor. The Aggressive investor's higher Return was the bonus gained for accepting the higher risk and volatility over the 30-year period. Each investor began with $100,000 in 1985 for our growth analysis. Without adjusting for taxes or management fees, there is a $2,665,415 difference between the Aggressive and Conservative ending values. It is important to note that the Conservative portfolio lost less than 8.1% in the worst year, versus a loss of 43% in the worst year for the Aggressive portfolio, yet the difference in return had a hugh impact on the overall wealth in 30 years.

The wealth inside the house is often omitted from investment comparisons. Given that a vast majority of our wealth is ending up in our houses, we need to make house wealth more visible as part of our overall financial planning. Let's take an example where you have a house worth $200,000, a mortgage o $75,000 - resulting in net equity of $125,000:

Current Situation	
Today's Value	**$200,000**
Current Mort-	**$75,000**
Net Equity	**$125,000**

Does this $125,000 house equity more closely resemble stocks, or bonds in terms of how it's return over time?

Stocks are shares of ownership sold by a corporation to raise money in exchange for dividends, voting rights, and other advantages. This is very different from your house investment.

Bonds are debts that an issuer owes to a holder based on a specific interest rate and maturity. Mortgages have an issuer (borrower) and a holder (lender), they have a specific interest rate and a maturity. The wealth located inside a house is more closely aligned bonds than stocks.

Let's look at a 30 year period of history to compare.

Borrowing Versus Stock and Bond Returns				**Housing Appreciation**
	30-year Fixed Rate	**30 Years of S&P500 Return**	**30 Year Long Bond***	
1986	10.19	18.67	15.30	2.92
1987	10.21	5.25	2.75	4.13
1988	10.34	12.73	7.89	3.70
1989	10.32	16.61	14.53	4.53
1990	10.13	31.69	8.96	4.58
1991	9.25	-3.10	16.00	0.50
1992	8.39	30.47	7.40	0.92
1993	7.31	7.62	9.75	0.30
1994	8.38	10.08	-2.92	0.82
1995	7.93	1.32	18.46	1.84
1996	7.81	37.58	3.64	0.90
1997	7.60	22.96	9.64	2.03
1998	6.94	33.36	8.70	3.00
1999	7.44	28.58	-.82	5.24
2000	8.05	21.04	11.63	6.97
2001	6.97	-9.10	8.43	7.52
2002	6.54	-11.89	10.26	7.34
2003	5.83	-22.1	4.10	10.60
2004	5.84	28.68	4.34	11.36
2005	5.87	4.91	2.43	16.27
2006	6.41	15.61	4.33	15.92
2007	6.34	5.48	6.97	1.04
2008	6.03	-36.55	5.24	-10.56
2009	5.04	25.94	5.93	-18.87
2010	4.69	14.82	6.54	-2.75
2011	4.45	2.10	7.84	-6.64
2012	3.66	15.89	4.22	-3.64
2013	3.98	32.15	-2.02	8.62
2014	4.17	13.52	5.97	12.25
2015	3.85	***1.38***	***.55***	***6.87***
	7.00%	11.86%	6.88%	4.26%
			*Barclay's US Ag Bond Index	*FreddieMac

If we compare the most recent 30-year historical cost of borrowing with the historical yield paid on bonds and stocks, we find the cost of borrowing and the interest paid on bonds track quite closely to one another. The 30-year fixed rate averaged 7.00%, while the long-term bond averaged 6.88%. It is clear that the cost of borrowing is closely correlated to the return on bonds.

What if we considered equity in your house as part of your bond portfolio and then compared your mix of investments?

If we include the $125,000 house equity (in our two prior examples) as part our bond investment - we shift the asset allocation percentage of stocks and bonds. Is this now really an Aggressive, Moderate or Conservative mix?

Aggressive?		**Moderate?**		**Conservative?**	
Stocks	$100,000	Stocks	$60,000	Stocks	$0
*Bonds	$125,000	Bonds	$165,000	Bonds	$225,000
$225,000		**$225,000**		**$225,000**	

***Bonds = Bond Investment + Net Equity in House**

In the above example, if you don't consider your house equity as part of your assets, you are likely not considering it as part of your asset allocation.

Let's try an example of how this might impact your real returns: Marvin and Judy Brown, both age 35, plan to purchase a $200,000 house with $200,000 from a recent inheritance. If they pay cash, they won't have to pay interest, and they can invest their savings each month. If they instead take out a $200,000 mortgage loan, they can invest their $200,000 from their inheritance. They are in a 32% state and federal tax bracket.

For their overall investment planning, the Browns are candidates for an Aggressive investment mix, because they don't plan to retire for at least 30 years. They make maximum contributions to their company sponsored 401(k). Their only other savings was a cash money market fund of $10,000. If their decision to locate $200,000 inside the house is compared to a diversified investment portfolio, how might it affect their wealth-building potential?

Impact To Net Worth Over Time

Prior to Inheritance		Option 1 - No Mortgage After Inheritance		Option 2 - Mortgage After Inheritance	
Aggressive Goal					
Stocks	$0	Stocks	$0	Stocks	$160,000
Bonds	$0	House	$200,000	House	$200,000
Assets:	$0	Assets:	$200,000	Assets:	$360,000
- Liabilities:	$0	- Liabilities:	$0	- Liabilities:	$160,000
Net Worth:	**$0**	**Net Worth:**	**$200,000**	**Net Worth:**	**$200,000**
Monthly Payment:			**$0**		**($933)**
Avg. Tax Savings:					**$298**
Avg. Net Payment:					**($635)**

	Option 1		Option 2
	Performance (1985 - 2015)		**Performance (1985 - 2015)**
	Avg. Annual Return:		**Avg. Annual Return:**
Stocks:	**11.86%**	**Stocks:**	**11.86%**
House:	**4.26%**	**House:**	**4.26%**
	Future Value:		**Future Value:**
Stocks:	**$2,151,415**	**Stocks:**	**$5,517,644**
House:	**$699,135**	**House:**	**$699,135**
Mortgage:	**$0**	**Mortgage:**	**-$160,000**
Payments:	**$0**	**Payment:**	**-$228,600**
Net	**$2,850,550**	**Net**	**$5,825,179**

If the Browns borrow $160,000, their payment of $933 in interest would provide average tax savings of $298. Their net cost averages $635 on a monthly after tax basis. If the Browns choose Option 1, we assume they pay cash for the house, and they invest $635 monthly in stocks for 30 years. For this example we'll use the 11.86% Return as an after tax growth rate. If the Browns choose Option 2, they would invest $40,000 in the house, borrowing the remaining $160,000 as a 7.00% interest only loan. They would place $160,000 that remains into stocks at the same assumed rate of return. We'll assume that they have to pay $635 each month for 30 years as an after tax interest payment, and their mortgage balance in 30 years will still be $160,000.

With no mortgage, the couple can invest $635 a month into stocks at 11.86%* while the house grows at 4.26%, creating future wealth of $2,850,550.

With a mortgage, the couple can invest $160,000 up front for 30 years at 11.86% while the house grows at 4.26%, they'll make payments of $228,600 (after tax) for their mortgage and still owe $160,000 in 30 years, but their future wealth is $5,825,179.

Assuming they retire after 30 years, at age 65, this diversification of their assets increased their net worth by $2,974,629. *While we don't know what average annual return will actually be over 30 years, you can begin to see the potential impact of diversification. Future stock returns may only be 8%, but future borrowing could be 4%, thereby still providing a spread for positive wealth creation.

Over time, you will probably want to adjust your own investment mix to reflect your age, your risk tolerance, and overall market trends. Your tolerance for risk will probably decrease as you approach retirement and have fewer years ahead to recover from losses. If your plan includes paying off your house before you retire, it will make sense to aim for an appropriate mix of bonds, and stocks to insure that you will have that flexibility. If your house is already paid off, it makes sense to consider how that wealth inside the house may be used in retirement. At 55 years old, you might plan to live in a house for another 30 years. Consider the impact of borrowing on those long term decisions.

If you find that too much of your savings is in bonds, after adding the house wealth to your calculations, you could move some of your existing bond portfolio into stocks. Or, you might stop making extra principal repayments on your mortgage as a way of rebalancing over time. You may even want to consider an interest-only mortgage that would allow you to increase employer-matched 401(k) investments. You could use a Reverse Mortgage to reduce your expenses in retirement.

If you find you have too little exposure to bonds, it might make more sense to invest in bonds than to prepay all or part of your mortgage, especially if you have limited current Liquidity. Remember, prepaying a mortgage does provide you a guaranteed interest savings (Return) based on your current EPR™. That's your bond like return that you'll either pay or earn.

The house wealth, if incorporated into your overall financial plan, may disturb the perceived diversity of your current investments. Consider your time horizon and risk tolerance before making a decision to leave the house wealth out of your long-term financial plan.

Summary of Key Learnings

- *Diversification offers the potential to earn the same Return with less overall risk.*

- *Wealth inside the house is often omitted in the overall financial planning process.*

- *Wealth inside the house reduces the amount of interest you pay. The net Return on this savings is very similar to the Return of having that same money invested in bonds, but with market risk.*

- *By viewing house wealth as part of the overall investment portfolio, you can get a better feel of how your money is functioning for long-term wealth development.*

Part II

The 7-Step Borrow Smart Solution

Now that we've established the Foundations for Borrowing Smart, you can begin to take more informed action if you borrow now. Even if you were not able to absorb all of the concepts in Part I, we've incorporated those concepts into simple exercises to build your Borrow Smart strategy.

While the Foundations discussed in Part I are essential building blocks for your perspective on how you'll borrow, the 7-Step Solution will help you assess the merits of specific actions you may take now based on what is appropriate for your current, specific situation.

Your Current and Specific Needs

Each person has unique current and specific needs based on age, experience, risk tolerance and other factors. The only real constant is change. Changes in one's personal or financial life often warrant changes in personal borrowing or investment strategy. Therefore, it's always important to consider your current, specific needs by reviewing these 7-Steps any time you experience a personal or financial change.

For example, imagine that you have recently financed your new house with a 7-Year ARM. Then, you learn that your company will be transferring you next year to a new office in another state. Reviewing the Borrow Smart steps again you realize you could refinance to a 1-Year ARM and save over $4,000 in the next 12 months. From a change in job location to the birth of a baby, any major life event could change borrowing strategies that impact your saving strategies. Over a 30 to 60-Year period, even small decisions can have a tremendous impact on your wealth creation if you take action to employ that savings to build new wealth.

Remember, good decisions, just like bad ones, compound over time.

Let's Play a Game

Imagine that you are playing a game with a goal of accumulating the most wealth possible based on your personal cash flow. In this game, you are given a variety of products that you can use to transport your cash; we'll call these products "buckets." You can choose which buckets to fill each month from your "faucet" of current cash flow.

Each bucket has different aspects of Safety, Liquidity, and Return that make them more efficient, or less efficient, in their role. This efficiency relates to the leaks associated with each bucket. Some buckets have more leaks than others and take longer to fill. Some leaks are obvious, and some are not.

Given that personal cash flow is relatively fixed for most of us, you have to decide whether to find and repair the current leaks or to continue to swap one bucket for the next, always hoping for a better bucket. You will come to quickly realize that the bucket you have today fills more quickly when the leaks are repaired, regardless of what kind of bucket you are filling.

Start Playing, Learn the Rules Later

The first time you played tic-tac-toe, did you win or lose? How about the second time? I'd guess that the first time someone showed you the game, you probably lost. I'd also bet that the second or third time you played, you were less likely to lose. Eventually, when both players understand the rules of tic-tac-toe, the winner is the one who can maintain their focus.

Like tic-tac-toe, the rules of managing wealth in the house are very much within your reach. Once you realize that you're playing a game, you'll be more likely to want to understand the rules. You can spend your entire life playing a game without realizing it. Or, you can learn the rules and choose to play with a higher degree of financial awareness.

Step 1

Product

The "Product" you select guarantees the interest rate that meets your current, specific borrowing needs. Selecting a loan Product is about risk management. It involves estimating how long you will keep your house AND your current mortgage. Many Americans have a fixed-rate mortgage that extends over a period of 15 years or longer, even if they continue to move or refinance every 3 to 5 years. Typically, the longer the lender guarantees the fixed portion of your loan Product, the higher the interest rate they charge. Thus, you could end up paying for more risk protection than you actually need.

When choosing a loan Product, there are two primary questions to ask yourself, "How many years do I expect to have this house?" and "How many years do I expect to have this loan?" Your decision on how long to secure your interest rate would be the shortest of these two periods. To get the lowest rate with the least risk, you want to fix the interest rate for no longer than necessary. If you know your time frame, you can choose a Product that provides the right amount of interest rate protection at the lowest possible cost.

If you expect to live in a house for 5 years, then you should first consider a Product that protects your interest rate risk for at least 5 years. The Product should reflect how long you will need a specific loan and subsequently, how long you want protection from interest rate movements.

What Is Interest Rate Risk?

Interest rate risk is the risk involved in the rise and fall of interest rates over time. Given that most borrowers can easily adapt to falling rates, you should be most concerned with rising interest rates that expose you to higher payments. Although a long-term fixed-rate mortgage can protect you from rising interest rates, it can also result in unnecessarily high monthly payments. Adjustable rate Products tend to have lower interest rates than fixed-rate loans, but they are subject to more interest rate risk. Either way, you face some risk. Fortunately, some loan products combine some of the advantages of each approach.

Own a Crystal Ball?

You probably do not know exactly when you will be moving out of your current house, unless you have already sold it and set a specific closing date. As soon as you sell your house and buy another house, however, it is time to start asking yourself how long you will stay in your next house and keep the new loan.

When thinking about your time frame, what number comes first to mind? Three years? Eight years? I've found that the first reaction to the time-frame question is often the most reliable one. If you think too much about your answer, you might get off course.

If no specific number comes to mind, is there a range of time in which you expect to stay in the house – say, 8 to 10 years? You want the interest rate you pay to be as low as possible while still providing protection from interest rate increases. The key is to select the Product that best suits your time frame.

What if you have no idea how long you will stay in the house but you don't expect to be there for the rest of your life? Seven years might be a reasonable estimate. The National Association of Realtors often cites 5.7 years as the average life of an existing house or loan transaction. The Joint Center for Housing Studies at Harvard University shows the median age of a mortgage loan refinanced since 1993 as only 3.2 years. Why so low? Because people refinance more often during periods of falling interest rates. Also, our increased job location flexibility and ease of accessing low-interest loans seems to reduce our dependence on the 30-year fixed as the primary Product for interest rate protection.

How Might Your Product Decision Affect Your Wealth?

The Wall Street Journal once quoted former Federal Reserve Chairman Alan Greenspan asking, "How is it possible that Americans are unwittingly transferring a tremendous amount of their personal wealth away unnecessarily?" Greenspan was referring to the fact that more than 90% of all loans being serviced in the U.S. are extended fixed-rate mortgages, yet the average time that homeowners keep a mortgage is decreasing.

Consider the hypothetical example of Lisa and Joe Thompson, proud parents of one-year-old twins. They buy their first house at age 30. Based on their parents' advice, they obtain a 30-year fixed mortgage. At age 37, they sell the house and move to a larger house with more space for their growing family. Again, they obtain a 30-year mortgage. At age 43, they sell that house and buy an even larger house with a big garage and a family room for their teenagers. At age 50, they decide to accept jobs in a different city after their children have left for college. At age 57, they move again to pursue a new business opportunity during their peak earning years. At 64, they decide to downsize into a smaller house with less upkeep and maintenance as they prepare for retirement. By age 73, they are fully retired, and they purchase a townhouse near their grandchildren. This also frees up enough funds to purchase a condo at the beach. With each new house, they obtain a new 30-year mortgage. At age 80, Joe develops a heart condition that entails unexpected medical expenses and makes travel difficult. They sell the condo to help pay uncovered medical costs. At 87, Lisa becomes a widow, sells the townhouse, and moves in with her daughter to help stretch her remaining savings.

Is it possible that some life changing event will occur every 7 years that might change your housing or financing needs. There will undoubtedly be periods when Lisa and Joe would benefit from refinancing their mortgage. Their parents' well-meaning advice to secure a 30-year fixed loan doesn't consider the mobility of many of today's borrowers. It also fails to consider the wide range of lending programs now available for various borrowing needs. If the Thompsons had realized their 30-year loan Product would end up being replaced every 7 years, they may have chosen an "ARM" which stands for Adjustable Rate Mortgage, as a more suitable choice.

In the preceding example, a 7-Year intermediate ARM typically provides a lower interest rate than a comparable long-term fixed loan, with no interest risk during each 7-Year period. Assuming an average interest-rate savings of 1% and an average mortgage balance of $157,000 over their 57 year time period, a 7-Year intermediate ARM for each house purchase would have saved the Thompsons an average of $130.83 per month. That amount invested over 57 years at an average Return of 6% could have grown to $771,617, almost 5 times the amount originally borrowed.

The 7-Step Borrow Smart Solution helps you get the right initial borrowing solution to minimize your cost of ownership over time. How can having the right Product help you pay off your house years early? Lisa and Joe might have saved $130.83 per month for 57 years just by choosing a different loan product. If that amount were applied monthly toward paying off their mortgage of $157,000, they could have paid it off in 21.5 years.

If you were to choose the right loan Product to 'Borrow Smart' over your lifetime, you might find that this one Step of a suitable Product could provide you savings that exceeds the amount your borrow over time.

Today's Loan Products

Although lenders claim to offer hundreds of loan program options, a majority of loans fall into the three simple categories: Short Term ARM products (3 years or less), Intermediate Fixed ARM products (5 to 10 years), and Long-Term fixed products (more than 10 years).

Loan Product Groups		
Short Term ARM	**Intermediate Fixed ARM**	**Long Term Fixed**
1 mo. ARM	5 yr. ARM	15 yr. Fixed
6 mo. ARM	7 yr. ARM	20 yr. Fixed
12 mo. ARM	10 yr. ARM	30 yr. Fixed
3 yr. ARM		40 yr. Fixed

A 5-Year ARM means that the interest rate is fixed for 5 years and then adjusts in accordance with market interest rates starting in the 6th year. The duration of the ARM loan is typically 30 years. The duration of the loan, or amortization period, is the number of years before the loan must be paid off in full. Let's look closely at the 3 product groups.

Short Term ARM Products provide a fixed interest rate for a relatively short period of time, usually ranging from 1 month to 3 years. These loans are suitable for borrowers who need interest rate protection for a brief period, or for borrowers who are willing to exchange interest rate volatility for potentially lower rates. The Short Term ARM is an aggressive Product approach. The borrower shoulders the burden of the interest volatility in exchange for what could be a lower interest rate.

Intermediate Fixed ARM Products provide a fixed interest rate for longer than a Short Term ARM. They are generally for borrowers who need interest rate protection for 5 to 10 years. Often they are also suitable for those who are unsure how long they'll need a particular mortgage but want a measured degree of interest rate protection. The Intermediate Fixed ARM is a moderate Product approach. The borrower shoulders the burden of the interest volatility only after a fixed period of time.

Long-Term Fixed Products provide a single interest rate for the duration of the loan, which could be anywhere from 15 to 40 years. This type of loan is generally best for those who do not expect to move or refinance for an extended period of time, usually 15 or more years. If you have a fixed-rate loan and you need to access wealth in the house, you would use an equity line of credit. The Long Term Fixed is a conservative Product approach. The borrower shoulders no interest volatility during the term of the loan.

PRODUCT RISK PYRAMID

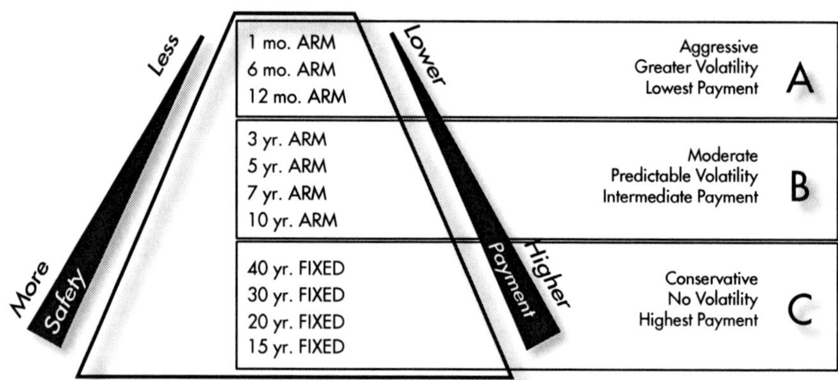

Many homeowners have a 30-year fixed mortgage. Borrowers often choose this option because they are concerned about the risk of rising interest rates. While that is a valid risk, an ARM offers similar protection for the fixed portion of its term. A 5-Year ARM, for example, provides a fixed rate for 5 years. In that sense, it is identical to the first 5 years of a 30-year fixed, except that the ARM typically has a lower interest rate. If you sell your house or refinance any time during the first five years, you are most likely better off with a 5-Year ARM. If you end up staying in the house for 7 years, you will have interest rate risk only during years 6 and 7. Increases in the interest rate of an ARM after the fixed period are usually limited in some way by interest rate caps.

In choosing a loan Product, you want to take as little unmeasured risk as possible, but you don't want to play it so safe that you lose money unnecessarily. In our prior example, the 30-year fixed loan for Lisa and Joe Thompson had no interest rate risk, but Safety came with a substantial cost.

Life Events / Market Changes

The first step in the Borrow Smart process is to choose a loan Product that covers your interest rate risk for an appropriate time period. Changes in life often come more quickly than one expects. It is likely that several events in your life will have a meaningful impact on your specific house ownership needs. Consider the possibilities of marriage, job promotions, job loss, birth of a child, birth of more children, divorce, career change, downsizing, death of a family member, purchase of a second house, inheritance, college costs, retirement, nursing care, and other events and needs. In addition to life changes, remember that since 1993 the median age of a mortgage loan refinanced was under 3 years. Many life events can change your current situation and alter your mortgage Product needs, not to mention external market driven events in the economy.

Events and Their Potential Impacts	
New Career	sell house – buy house – remodel house office
Death of Spouse	sell house – buy house – remodel home office
Interest Rates Increase	refinance to fixed rate
Interest Rates Decrease	refinance to lower rate – cash out
Inheritance	buy house – pay off house
Children in College	refinance cash out – equity line credit
Parent Illness	refinance cash out – equity line credit
Empty Nest	smaller house – remodel
Children Finish College	smaller house – remodel – second house
Retirement	smaller house – remodel – second house
Nursing Care	smaller house – remodel – second house
Assisted Living	sell house – rent house

In this sample list of life events, you can imagine how events trigger a need for changes in housing and related liabilities. The growing ease and declining cost of the loan transaction itself empowers the house owner to make rapid changes in their borrowing practices to capitalize on small interest rate fluctuations. Additionally, new loan Products that closely align with changing financial needs will become available that create other opportunities.

In the following exercise, we'll give you a simple way to identify the Product that best fits your current needs. The right product is the first step toward minimizing the cost of borrowing, which in turn allows you to increase your lifestyle today, or your savings for tomorrow.

Product Work Table

Question 1		
When you think about risk, are you?		
(Conservative)	(Moderate)	(Aggressive)
☐	☐	☐

Question 2a		
How many years do I expect to have this house?		
(Short Term)	(Intermediate Term)	(Long Term)
☐ <1 ☐ 2-3	☐ 4-5 ☐ 6-7 ☐ 8-10	☐ 11-15 ☐ 16-20 ☐ 20-40

Question 2b		
How many years do I expect to have this loan?		
(Short Term)	(Intermediate Term)	(Long Term)
☐ <1 ☐ 2-3	☐ 4-5 ☐ 6-7 ☐ 8-10	☐ 11-15 ☐ 16-20 ☐ 20-40

In your answers above, circle the shortest term you specified above for either 2a or 2b - that will be your Target Term.

- *If your answer to Question 1 is Conservative, circle the term to the right of your Target Term.*
- *If your answer to Question 1 is Moderate, do nothing with your Target Term.*
- *If your answer to Question 1 is Aggressive, circle the term to the left of your Target Term.*

For example, if you chose 4-5 yrs for Question 2a and 20-40 yrs for 2b, then the term of 4-5yrs under Question 2a is your Target Term. You would circle that. If you chose Conservative for Question 1 then move one to the right of 2a (given that 2a was the shortest of the two answers) and use 6–7 yrs. Round up to the highest. Therefore, you should choose a 7-Year Intermediate Fixed ARM as your Product.

If you are meeting with a lender for a purchase or refinance, you now know the Product you need for interest rate protection. The 7-Year Intermediate Fixed ARM will provide you a fixed interest rate for 7 years before it will adjust, and should provide you the lowest cost relative to your desired risk. In this example if you thought you would have this house for 4-5 years, a 7 year ARM gives you fixed interest for 7 years, exceeding your needs while giving you a lower interest rate than a comparable Long Term Fixed Product.

You would only opt for a Product with a longer period of fixed interest rate protection if the lender offers a 7-Year Intermediate Fixed ARM and a 10-Year Intermediate Fixed ARM at the same interest rate, all other factors being equal, you should take the 10-Year Intermediate Fixed ARM to get longer protection for the same rate.

Compare the payment you would have paid for a comparable 30-year fixed mortgage. This is the amount you might add to your monthly savings, or use to prepay your new mortgage. ▪

Step 2

Payment

"Payment" refers to the approach you will take to repay your mortgage over time that best fits your current specific borrowing needs. There are essentially three ways to repay a mortgage loan:

Amortizing	Interest-only	Negative amortizing

An amortizing payment is a planned transfer of wealth toward the repayment of borrowing by combining monthly principal and interest. An interest-only payment returns only the interest due the lender with no repayment of the remaining loan balance. A negative amortizing payment may be less than the actual interest owed, or such that the interest increases the outstanding mortgage balance.

Amortizing

The traditional mortgage loan repayment approach is to repay by amortizing the loan over a fixed period. The word 'amortize' stems from the Old French amortir, amortiss - "to bring to death". An amortizing loan is paid monthly, with a portion of the total payment allocated to interest and the remainder allocated toward principal such that the loan is 'terminated' at a specific time. The lender retains the interest portion as their return, and the portion allocated to principal is what pays down the remaining mortgage balance to $0. Based on the term of your loan (traditionally 30 years), the lender calculates the amount of principal and interest you need to pay each month in order to systematically pay off the loan during the term.

Year 1 - Amortizing Loan of $160,000*					
	Payments	**Interest**	**Principal**	**Balance**	**Tax Savings**
Month 1	$1,064.48	933.33	$131.15	$159,869	$326.67
Month 2	$1,064.48	932.57	$131.92	$159,737	$326.40
Month 3	$1,064.48	931.80	$132.69	$159,604	$326.13
Month 4	$1,064.48	931.02	$133.46	$159,471	$325.86
Month 5	$1,064.48	930.25	$134.24	$159,337	$325.59
Month 6	$1,064.48	929.46	$135.02	$159,202	$325.31
Month 7	$1,064.48	928.68	$135.81	$159,066	$325.04
Month 8	$1,064.48	927.88	$136.60	$158,929	$324.76
Month 9	$1,064.48	927.09	$137.40	$158,792	$324.48
Month 10	$1,064.48	926.29	$138.20	$158,654	$324.20
Month 11	$1,064.48	925.48	$139.01	$158,515	$323.92
Month 12	$1,064.48	924.67	$139.82	$158,375	$323.63
Totals	**$12,773**	**$11,149**	**$1,625**	**$158,375**	**$3,901**
Year 30	**$383,214**	**$223,214**	**$160,000**	**$0**	**$78,124**
**30-year fixed at 7% w/ 35% marginal tax bracket*					

The lender benefits from interest earned. The lender relies on the initial down payment, the decreasing principal balance, and possible appreciation in the value of the house as collateral. If you had a 30-year loan of $160,000 at 7%, your monthly payment would be $1,064. After 30 years, you would have paid total payments of $383,214. Your interest over and above the principal would total $223,214, or ($383,214 total payments - $160,000 principal paid = $223,214 interest).

If your interest were tax deductible over the life of the loan (based on a 35% annual state and federal bracket), you would have saved $78,124 in taxes. Your total interest payments of $223,214 (minus) $78,124 in taxes saved would yield net interest payments of $145,090 to pay the mortgage balance down to $0. Thus, in the amortizing payment example, the net interest cost of the $160,000 loan is approximately 91% of the principal amount originally borrowed.

Interest-Only

The interest-only (non-amortizing) mortgage requires a monthly payment of the interest due on the loan, but no monthly repayment of the principal. The amount of principal owed is frozen during the entire life of the loan. If you borrow $160,000 with a 30-year interest-only loan, the principal balance would be $160,000 after 30 years.

In an interest-only loan, the lender relies on the security of your initial down payment and possible appreciation in the value of your house as collateral. Since monthly repayments do not include any of the principal, the lender cannot benefit from a decreasing principal balance. Over the course of an interest-only loan, you are required to make no payments toward the principal balance. If the term of the interest-only period is 30 years, your loan balance could remain the same for 30 years.

A loan can also be part interest-only and part amortized. For example, a 7 Year Interest Only ARM might have interest rate fixed for 7 years, and the require interest-only for the first 7-10 years. Your principal would remain the same during the first 7-10 years. After that, the monthly payments would include principal and interest so that you make sure you pay off the full loan balance within 30 years.

An interest-only loan has lower monthly payments than a comparable amortizing loan, because no principal is included in the payment. However, the total amount of interest paid over the lifetime of an interest-only loan is higher than in an amortizing loan, because the loan balance does not decrease over time. If you have a $160,000 interest only loan, you are paying interest on $160,000 during the interest only portion of the loan.

Year 1 - Interest Only Loan of $160,000*

	Payments	Interest	Principal	Balance	Tax Savings
Month 1	$933.33	$933.33	$0.00	$160,000	$326.67
Month 2	$933.33	$933.33	$0.00	$160,000	$326.67
Month 3	$933.33	$933.33	$0.00	$160,000	$326.67
Month 4	$933.33	$933.33	$0.00	$160,000	$326.67
Month 5	$933.33	$933.33	$0.00	$160,000	$326.67
Month 6	$933.33	$933.33	$0.00	$160,000	$326.67
Month 7	$933.33	$933.33	$0.00	$160,000	$326.67
Month 8	$933.33	$933.33	$0.00	$160,000	$326.67
Month 9	$933.33	$933.33	$0.00	$160,000	$326.67
Month 10	$933.33	$933.33	$0.00	$160,000	$326.67
Month 11	$933.33	$933.33	$0.00	$160,000	$326.67
Month 12	$933.33	$933.33	$0.00	$160,000	$326.67
Totals	**$11,200**	**$11,200**	**$0**	**$160,000**	**$3,920**
Year 30	**$336,000**	**$336,000**	**$0**	**$160,000**	**$117,600**

**30-year fixed at 7% w/ 35% marginal tax bracket*

If you had a 30-year interest-only loan of $160,000 at 7%, your monthly payment would be $933. After 30 years, you would have paid a total of $336,000 in interest, and no principal. If your interest were tax-deductible (based on a 35% state and federal bracket), you would have saved $117,600 in taxes. Your total interest payments of $336,000 (minus) $117,600 in taxes saved equals a net interest cost of $218,400 to maintain the mortgage balance of $160,000. Thus, in the interest only payment example, the net interest cost of the $160,000 loan is approximately 137% of the principal amount originally borrowed. This is a great deal higher than the amortizing payment.

The amortizing loan had total after tax payments of $305,090 to pay the loan balance to $0, while the interest-only loan had total after tax payments of $218,400 to maintain the balance of $160,000. This difference in cost – $305,090 minus $218,400 – is $86,690 in cash flow savings to the interest-only borrower. This $86,690 over 360 months is equivalent to $240.80 in average monthly cash flow.

In some cases an interest only will make the house easier to afford, but at the cost of not reducing the mortgage balance, and it's a little more like leasing a house instead of buying one. For some it can be a financial planning strategy. If you invested the $240.80 payment difference in an investment earning a 7% after tax return for the 30-year period, it would grow to $293,769.

At the end of the mortgage term you could pay off the loan balance of $160,000, and keep $133,769 in net savings. If you reduced your $218,400 interest cost by the remaining $133,769 in your investment account, your net interest cost would be only $84,631. That's 52% of the $160,000 principal amount originally borrowed. This greatly reduces your cost of borrowing, but puts you in a position of actively managing the equity investment over time - you as the borrower take on the Market Risk and the Discipline Risk of managing your savings. Let's see what this might look like in an example.

Amortizing Fixed Repayment versus Interest Only Payment

Couple A and Couple B each buy their first $200,000 house at age 30. Both couples finance $160,000 with a 30-year fixed mortgage. Both couples live in their house for 30 years, realize a 2% annual appreciation, and are in a 35% marginal tax bracket. The only difference is that Couple A chooses an amortizing loan, and Couple B chooses an interest-only loan, planning to invest their savings.

Each month, Couple A makes principal and interest payments, while Couple B makes interest-only payments and saves the cash flow and tax savings in a separate investment account. The effect on each couple's future savings might look like the following:

Potential Payment Impact: Amortizing versus Interest Only							
Years	Future House Value	Future Mortgage Balance	Total Payments Paid	Total Interest Paid	Total Tax Savings	Total Investment Savings	Future Net Worth
$200,000 house with a 30-year fixed mortgage of $160,000 at 7% (AMORTIZING)							
1 - 30	$364,242	$0	$383,214	$226,815	$78,124	N/A	+$59,303
$200,000 house with a 30-year fixed mortgage of $160,000 at 7% (INTEREST ONLY)							
1 - 30	$662,700	$160,000	$336,000	$336,000	$117,600	$293,769*	+$279,611
*assumes 7% after tax return with principal and tax savings invested monthly							

The choice of payment option can have a real effect on future net worth. In the above example, the interest-only loan helps generate $220,308 in additional net worth for Couple B (assuming a 7% net after tax return on the monthly investment of their $240.80), but only because the net principal and tax savings were invested at a Return that exceeded the cost of borrowing. To calculate the net worth, we take the Future House Value - Future Mortgage Balance - Total Interest Paid + Total Tax Savings + Total Investment Savings = Future Net Worth.

The financial reward for the interest-only option has Market Risk and Discipline Risk of having to invest the savings. If the couple earns a lower rate or return, or spends the savings, they could end up in a worse position.

In general, an amortizing loan may be the better option if you require the discipline of planned repayment available through an amortizing loan, or if the guaranteed EPR™ of placing money in your house is higher than the EPR™ of having that money located outside the house. If the EPR™ of locating that money outside your house is higher, then an interest-only loan may be your best bet if you can manage that savings yourself.

There are four common ways to pay off the balance of an interest-only mortgage loan:

- *Using proceeds from the eventual sale of the house.*

- *Using an outside source, such as an investment account set up specifically for this purpose, where the savings from the interest-only payment and taxes are deposited monthly.*

- *Paying the interest only portion throughout the year, and then making lump sum payments at specific times throughout the year. Commissioned sales people like this option as it gives them a lower monthly minimum payment, and the flexibility to make larger lump sum payments to still rapidly pay down the mortgage balance.*

- *Selecting a product that amortizes at a certain point during the term of the loan. For example, a 30-year loan might be interest-only for the first 10 years and amortized over the next 20 years. During the last 20 years, monthly payments would be for both principal and interest, so that the loan would be paid in full by the end of the 30-year term. This gives a young couple 10 years to increase their income earning potential before they have a larger required payment.*

Compared with amortizing, the interest-only repayment approach provides the borrower with greater cash flow, higher potential tax deductions, and greater flexibility regarding future loan repayment. To benefit, however, the borrower must have the discipline to invest the savings. It might seem like "free" money, but it's not. If you spend the savings created by an interest-only mortgage, the interest-only option will increase your net cost of borrowing.

Negative Amortizing

The negative amortizing mortgage is typically associated with a reverse mortgage, certain home equity lines, or other unique products that allow monthly interest to accrue and increase the outstanding mortgage balance each month. The interest, like in an interest only mortgage, is due each month. However, a negative amortizing product provides flexibility. The borrower may choose to make the interest payment in full, or defer the payment to a point and time in the future where it will be paid in full. Any interest not paid in the month due, is added to the outstanding loan balance, negatively amortizing the loan.

The lender relies on the security of the initial down payment and the possibility of appreciation in the value of the house. The lender has less risk in a standard amortizing loan as the decreasing principal balance increase the equity inside the house. The lender's risk increases any time the loan balance increases, as such negative amortizing loans may have a higher interest rate to reflect the lender's increase risk. Over the course of a negative amortizing loan, you are required to make no payments toward the principal balance until the loan cap is reached, if there is one. At that point, your payment will increase to at least to the point where interest or interest and principal are due to reduce some portion of the principal.

Year 1 - Negative Amortizing Loan of $160,000*

	Payments	Interest	Principal	Balance	Tax Savings
Month 1	$0	$933.33	$0	$160,933	$326.67
Month 2	$0	$938.78	$0	$161,872	$328.03
Month 3	$0	$944.25	$0	$162,816	$329.40
Month 4	$0	$949.76	$0	$163,766	$330.77
Month 5	$0	$955.30	$0	$164,721	$332.16
Month 6	$0	$960.87	$0	$165,682	$333.55
Month 7	$0	$966.48	$0	$166,648	$334.95
Month 8	$0	$972.12	$0	$167,620	$336.36

Month 9	$0	$977.79	$0	$168,598	$337.78
Month 10	$0	$983.49	$0	$169,582	$339.21
Month 11	$0	$989.23	$0	$170,571	$340.64
Month 12	$0	$995.00	$0	$171,566	$342.08
Totals	**$0**	**$11,566**	**$0**	**$171,566**	**$4,048****
Year 30	$0	$1,138,640	$0	$1,298,639	$398,524

**payment at 7% base rate w/ 35% marginal tax bracket*
*** interest isn't typically deductible until actually paid by the borrower*

Consider a reverse mortgage of $160,000 at 7%. If the loan payment is based on a 7% rate, the required monthly payment would be $933.33 for the first month. The actual interest of $933.33 is the same as the interest-only mortgage we discussed, but the borrower can choose to defer the $933 and that amount is added to the existing balance. In the following month, the interest-only payment grows to $938.78, to reflect the increasing balance.

Thus, the balance will grow each month, until the cap is reached. In some specialty products this could be based on a time frame, or a loan-to-value ratio. In the reverse mortgage scenario, it's based on the death of the borrower, with no specific time limit.

The long-term tax and cash-flow effects of negative amortization can be complex, so you should consult a tax, financial or lending advisor trained in this type of payment option. The reverse mortgage, or speciality negative amortizing product solution can be great for those needing control over their cash flow.

Alternatives for paying off the principal in a negative amortizing loan are similar to those for paying off an interest-only loan. The borrower may:

- *Use proceeds from the eventual sale of the house.*

- *Use an outside source, such as an investment account, or insurance policy set up specifically for mortgage repayment.*

- *Through future lump sum payments at the option of the borrower.*

The negative amortizing payment approach could help you maximize cash flow, increase potential tax deductions, and maximize flexibility in determining when to repay the loan. The compounding interest works against you in a negative amortizing loan, increasing the burden on the borrower to earn a compounding growth rate that exceeds this cost of borrowing. One positive can be the compounding growth of the property value. If the property value in increasing, that can help to offset the impact of the negative interest loan balance increases.

Pros and Cons of Amortizing

PROS

- *The amortizing loan balance decreases in a predictable way, over a set period of time. It provides the lowest interest cost on a guaranteed basis.*

- *A repayment to an amortizing loan is guaranteed to save the EPR™ interest as the principal is paid down.*

- *The amortizing repayment system requires less financial discipline than alternative payment methods.*

- *For those who have difficulty saving money, the difficulty of accessing wealth in the house can make the house repayment a forced savings plan.*

CONS

- *Monthly payments reduce the loan balance and subsequent interest paid. Therefore, itemized deductions decrease over time.*

- *Use and control of principal that could have been invested to earn interest at a higher return is unavailable.*

- *Access to principal comes only from selling the house, or borrowing against the property.*

Pros and Cons of an Interest-Only Loan

PROS

- *Since the loan balance does not decrease during the interest only period, the amount of interest that is tax-deductible does not decrease during the interest only period.*

- *Principal payments may be invested for a higher target return to increase wealth, or provide additional liquidity and reduce the overall cost of borrowing.*

- *This external wealth allows a prepayment of mortgage principal at a time of the borrowers choosing that may be financially more appealing.*

- *Increased cash flow and liquidity allow the borrower to make principal repayments when they deem them appropriate, or repay the mortgage at a time of their choosing.*

CONS

- *Money saved by not paying down the principal could be spent, greatly increasing the net interest cost of borrowing.*

- *Investing the savings under unfavorable market conditions could cause a loss of wealth.*

- *At the end of the interest-only period, the borrower may not be ready, prepared, or financially able to handle the change in payment.*

Pros and Cons of a Negative Amortizing Loan

PROS

- *House payments are optional, greatly increasing current cash flow, liquidity, and use and control of money for other opportunities.*

- *The loan balance increases, which helps maximize the tax-deductibility of payments made at some point in the future.*

- *Greater tax planning efficiencies are available to help offset other gains by planning refinances to coincide with other financial events.*

CONS

- *Greater financial self-discipline is required to make effective use of the money saved by having low monthly payments.*

- *Because payment calculations are complex, it is possible to misunderstand the workings of the product and create unexpected financial challenges in the future. This isn't the case with the Reverse Mortgage which has safety measures built in.*

- *Steep payment increases at the end of the negative amortization period could cause financial cash flow challenges. This isn't the case with the Reverse Mortgage which has safety measures built in.*

Choosing a Payment

Once you understand your loan payment options, you can choose a Payment that reflects your current specific needs. I generally recommend balancing flexibility with discipline to find the right mix for your current needs.

I have found that choosing an interest-only loan or a negative amortization loan can be either a very positive or a very negative experience. If you believe your potential EPR™ outside the house is higher than your EPR™ of money inside the house, then it makes sense financially to build wealth outside the house and repay the house at a future time of your choice. However, if your EPR™ is greater for money inside the house, then an amortizing loan may be your better option. In general, amortizing is a conservative path, while interest-only is a moderate path. Negative-amortizing is for those who wish to pursue an aggressive path toward borrowing and can afford the added interest rate volatility of a niche product, or have chosen a Reverse Mortgage to maximize their financial needs in their later years.

Let's use the following process to identify the Payment type that best first your current needs.

Payment Work Table

Question 1	
Which of the following apply to you? (check all that apply)	
☐	I have the discipline to save.
☐	I am willing to find an advisor for assistance, or I have the experience to direct the savings myself.
☐	I would be comfortable with not knowing the exact date that I'll pay off my house mortgage.
☐	I don't mind managing the market and discipline risk of keeping my wealth outside the house.
☐	I have sufficient income to support interest volatility that could increase or decrease my monthly payment.

Question 2	
Which of the following best describes your current specific needs relative to cash flow?	
Lower Payment Higher Tax Deduction Pay Little or No Principal ☐	Higher Payment Lower Tax Deduction Pay Principal Monthly ☐

Now, add up your score using the table below by referencing the answers to the two prior questions.

Score 1 point for each box checked in Question 1.	Points: ______.
For Question 2:	**(Circle One)**
I selected: Lower Payment Higher Tax Deduction Pay Little or No Principal	**+ 2 points.**
I selected: Higher Payment Lower Tax Deduction Pay Principal Monthly	**+ 1 point.**
Total Points:	______. **(max 7 points)**

If your score totals 4 or less, stick with an amortizing loan Payment until your current specific needs change. If your score is 5 or higher, an interest-only loan Payment could prove a financially sound move.

If you are aware of specific niche loan product that offers negative amortizing* solutions, consider them only if you score a 6 or higher in this survey.

*If you are over age 62, a reverse mortgage could be a safe way to maximize your payment flexibility in retirement. Your Product choices will be limited, but your Payment flexibility will be very high. You could skip the remaining 7 Step process and begin your Reverse Mortgage research to identify if that's a clear choice for you now.

At this point you should have a Product, and a Payment strategy, maybe you've selected a 5 Year Product, and an Amortizing Payment. Next we'll determine your Availability.

Step 3

Availability

"Availability" refers to the maximum amount you would be qualified to borrow for your mortgage. It is not the Amount of money you *should* borrow (covered in Step 4). Rather, it is the maximum amount you are allowed to borrow.

Availability varies over time. It is based on your current specific situation, and it involves the 4 C's in Chapter 5: Character, Capacity, Collateral, and Credit.

Once you have chosen your Product (Step 1) and Payment (Step 2), then Availability (Step 3) will help you understand how much you can borrow. Given that lending guidelines often change, you will want to consult with a qualified lender to calculate your exact Availability for a given loan.

The 4 C's influence how much you are allowed to borrow to purchase or refinance a house based on lender underwriter guidelines. While you may be qualified to borrow more than the purchase price, we'll assume that Availability is always capped at 100% of the purchase price. For a refinance, we'll assume it's capped at 100% of the property value. Some government loans will allow financing above 100% of the property value when you finance in closing costs, fees, etc.

Availability When Purchasing

Let's say you are buying a $200,000 house, and you have $40,000 for a down payment. You would need to borrow $160,000 at a minimum. We want to know how much of the $200,000 you could borrow. That number is what we call Availability. If you are qualified to borrow up to $200,000, then $200,000 is your Availability.

Availability is the amount you are allowed to access through borrowing. Once you know your Availability, you can determine the Amount you will actually borrow. That will be the focus of Step 4.

Let's say you sold your previous residence and received $150,000 at the closing. Let's also say you plan to buy a new house for $300,000. First you would need to find out how much of the $300,000 you are allowed to borrow based on your current specific situation. The lender tells you that your Availability is 80% of the $300,000, or $240,000. You could choose to invest between $60,000 (the minimum required by the lender based on a $240,000 loan) and $150,000 (the maximum amount you have available for a down payment).

Availability When Refinancing

If you are refinancing your house, the maximum Availability would be its current value. Let's say you are refinancing a $200,000 house, and you have a current loan balance of $160,000. If the lender will allow you to borrow up to $200,000, then $200,000 would be your Availability. What matters is not that you have a current balance of $160,000, but that you are qualified to borrow $200,000.

From your personal wealth perspective, you need to know how much wealth is currently in your house and how much of it you are allowed to access. Considering Availability will help you stay aware of how wealth in the house – and access to that wealth – continues to fluctuate over time. Availability is affected by job changes, marriage, and other life events. Use the following tables to estimate your Availability.

Availability Work Table

Question 1		
Have the borrower or borrowers been in the same line of work, or profession, for at least 2 consecutive years?		
Borrower 1:	yes ☐	no ☐
Borrower 2:	yes ☐	no ☐

Question 2
What is the approximate combined value of your liquid assets, including bank accounts, mutual funds, CD's, and securities? (do not include retirement accounts)
$________________.

Question 3
What is your best estimate of your current credit score?
________.
(resources: freecreditreport.com / myfico.com)

Question 4	
What is your reported gross scheduled income for last year? If there is more than one borrower, record your combined gross scheduled income.	
$____________.	
multiply X 3	**multiply X 5**
= ____________.	= ____________.
Low Range	**High Range**

In Question 4, if your reported gross income last year was $100,000, then your Availability range is $300,000 to $500,000.

The degree to which you can access wealth at a reasonably low interest rate within your Availability range is a function of your answers to questions 1 through 3. We'll call this your Borrower Strength.

Remember, the four 4 C's of lending are Character (job), Capacity (income), Collateral (house equity and savings) and Credit (scores). Each of these C's affects the Availability of your house wealth.

Determining Borrower Strength

Now, add up your score using the table below by referencing the answers to the prior questions. The total is your Borrower Strength.

Score 1 point for each Yes in Question 1.	Points: ____. (maximum 2 points)
For Question 2:	(circle one)
My savings is currently $25,000 or more.	+ 1 point.
My savings is currently $125,000 or more.	+ 2 points.
For Question 3:	(circle one)
550 - 619	+ 1 point.
620 - 679	+ 2 points.
680 - 720	+ 3 points.
721 or higher	+ 4 points.
For Question 4:	(circle one)
My income is currently $40,000 or more.	+ 1 point
My income is currently $125,000 or more.	+ 2 points.
Borrow Strength Total Points:	____. (max 10 points)

If your Borrower Strength is 3 points or less:

- *Expect some real work on your part to find a lender.*
- *Also expect a relatively high interest rate.*
- *If you can secure a loan, your Availability will be at the low end of your Availability range.*

If your Borrower Strength is 4 or 5 points:

- *You can expect success in securing a loan, but the lender may set a relatively high interest rate, a high down payment, and other limitations.*
- *Expect your Availability to be toward the middle of your Availability range.*

If your Borrower Strength is 6 or higher:

- *You should have no problem securing a loan.*
- *The higher your score, the more likely you will see rate reductions and more flexible lending solutions.*
- *The lender might even offer to waive requirements for escrows or mortgage insurance. Your Availability will probably be toward the top of your Availability range.*

Availability Is Always Changing

Think about how your profile as a borrower might change over time and how this could affect your ability to borrow. Consider borrowing before you change careers, retire, begin divorce proceedings, or accept a commission-based job. Your Borrower Strength might be a perfect 10 today, but as soon as you retire, it might be 3 to 4 points lower.

The lender should be able to determine your exact Availability. As a general rule of thumb, however, you'll be able to access a multiple of your gross income with a degree of success that mirrors your current specific Borrower Strength. The role of Step 3 - Availability is to focus first on understanding that Availablility is always changing. Lose your job and your Availability might drop to $0. By focusing on Availability, you know your range of choice in working with a lender as to how much you put down, or decide to leave in the house each time you borrow.

Maybe you've selected a 5 Year Product, and an Amortizing Payment, and now you know your Availability is 80% of your current property value. With this knowledge, we'll want to determine the Amount that you'll borrow for this transaction.

Step 4

Amount

"Amount" refers to how much you borrow when you refinance or buy a house?

In the first three Steps, you chose an appropriate loan Product, decided which type of Payment would best balance function and flexibility, and estimated Availability based on your current borrowing strength. Step 4 helps you determine the Amount you will borrow.

The Amount you borrow may be either a function of simple necessity or a more complex matter of opportunity. It is always limited by Availability.

Remember, we define a debtor as someone who borrows solely out of necessity. A debtor is dependent on a lender to provide the Amount needed. When the lender offers an option to borrow more than you actually need, it presents an opportunity for a debtor to act as a Creditor. You are still a debtor in the strict sense of the word, however you borrow out of choice rather than necessity to capitalize on a financial opportunity.

If you need to borrow $50,000 to buy a house, but you have an option to borrow as much as $100,000, you may now choose to view the $50,000 that you could borrow based on the opportunities you have to utilize that money in different ways. Could investing that extra $50,000 in your own business give you a better return that putting down a larger down payment?

Our approach to Amount will look first at borrowing as a necessity, and secondly at borrowing as an opportunity.

Necessity versus Opportunity

Most of us have borrowed out of necessity for houses, cars, or other purchases. Let's say you borrow money from a local bank for your house at 6%, the same bank where you deposit your pay check each month. When you make a deposit to your checking account, you loan the use and control of your money to the bank for a little interest, say 2%. The bank as a professional creditor lends the use and control of their money back to you at 6%. The bank earns a 4% spread lending your money back to you. You borrowed out of necessity, while the bank provided a loan based on opportunity.

The house is one of the few assets you can purchase with borrowed money that might increase your net worth over time. The smarter you learn to borrow, the more flexibility you will have in your future borrowing decisions, and the greater the impact on your future wealth.

How dependent are you on borrowing for a specific purchase or refinance? If you must borrow all the money needed for a house, then the lender will determine your Amount for you based on your Availability.

If you do not need to borrow – if you can pay cash for a house – then the Amount you borrow is based solely on the Amount you determine based on your financial opportunity. This is true whether you are purchasing a new house or refinancing the house you already own.

If you need to borrow only a portion of the cost or value of the house, then you might consider yourself a debtor to the extent that you need to borrow and a creditor to the degree that you choose to borrow beyond your necessity.

Boosting Your Savings

As you increase your savings, you increase the opportunity to choose the Amount you borrow. If you are buying a $200,000 house, your borrowing flexibility will depend on:

1. The amount of liquid savings you have available.
2. Your Availability, as discussed Step 3.

If you are buying a house for $200,000 and you have $200,000 in liquid savings, then you have the option of paying cash. You may choose not to borrow. However, your borrowing flexibility depends on your Availability. The amount of cash savings you have does not guarantee that you can borrow a certain amount. Maximum flexibility requires liquid savings exceeding the $200,000 you need to borrow as well as the Availability to borrow $200,000 - that's the best of both worlds. The steps you take to Borrow Smart can help you more quickly achieve this flexibility.

The following table illustrates the degree to which you, rather than the lender, will determine your Amount.

House Value: $200,000 (purchase or refinance)			
Liquid Savings:	**> $200,000**	**< $200,000**	**< $0**
Borrowing Approach:	**Creditor**	**Debtor / Creditor**	**Debtor**
Amount Determined By:	**Opportunity / Availability**	**Necessity / Opportunity / Availability**	**Necessity / Availability**
Flexibility:	**< Higher**	**-**	**Lower >**

If you have little or no savings, then your choices in financing a house are likely to be determined by the Amount a lender will allow you to borrow.

Following Steps 1 – 3 can help you increase your savings, and your flexibility for future borrowing. If you utilized a 5 Year ARM and refinanced after 4 years, that interest savings could have been saved for a larger down payment on your next house.

What if you have a reasonable amount of savings, but not more than the purchase price (or the existing house value for a refinance)? Then, the purchase price (or house value) minus your available savings is the Amount you need to borrow – the Amount tied to necessity. If you have a $200,000 house and $50,000 in savings, you must borrow at least $150,000. If you borrow more than $150,000, you would do so based on opportunity to do something else with that money.

Borrowing as an Opportunity

If your current savings exceeds the purchase price (or house value), then your decision to borrow is often one of opportunity.

When determining the Amount of your loan that is tied to opportunity, you will want to consider the concepts we discussed in the earlier chapters. It's not just about Return, Safety, Liquidity, EPR™, Taxes; Leverage may also be a consideration. Those Foundations will help guide you toward an Amount that seems suitable, based on your current specific needs. Assuming you wish to focus on maximizing wealth when you have the flexibility to borrow based on an opportunity, not just necessity, your decision is basically whether to locate wealth inside or outside the house.

Imagine that you are buying a new house for $200,000, and you have $80,000 in savings. The lender tells you that your Availability is up to 100% of the purchase price on a VA loan, so you could borrow the entire $200,000 if you wanted. The entire $80,000 is tied to opportunity. The lender isn't requiring that you put that down out of necessity. Should you locate your $80,000 inside the house by making a $80,000 down payment? Or should you locate the $80,000 outside the house by borrowing $200,000 and leaving your $80,000 savings in an investment? A third choice, of course, would be to put part of the $80,000 inside the house and the rest of it outside the house. You could, for example, make a $40,000 down payment and borrow $160,000. You would then have $40,000 in savings to invest outside the house for greater liquidity, safety, return, tax savings, etc.

You have the luxury of choices, deciding where to locate your $80,000 is a decision of opportunity rather than necessity. How might you determine where to locate your $80,000?

Based on the concepts thus far, you might ask yourself the following questions: **Based on what I know today . . .**

- *Do I feel I would have a higher degree of Safety by having the wealth inside the house or outside the house?*

- *Do I think I would have a higher degree of Liquidity by having the wealth inside the house, or outside the house?*

- *Do I believe I would have a higher Return/EPR™ by having the wealth inside the house or outside the house?*

- *How would having the wealth inside the house, or outside the house impact my tax subsidy to offset the cost of borrowing?*

- *How much Leverage do I want to use, knowing that the degree to which I use Leverage is the degree to which I magnify my gains or my losses when borrowing?*

EPR™ in Action

EPR™ is a great tool for comparing the after-tax Return from investing money inside the house with the after-tax Return of investing it outside the house.

Here's an example of how to use it. For a mortgage with a rate of 6%, the EPR™ for someone in a 30% tax bracket would be around 4.20%. In deciding how much to borrow and how much to put into the house as a down payment, you would need to compare the EPR™ of putting money inside the house (which is a guaranteed investment) with the EPR™ of investing money outside the house (which may or may not be guaranteed). You know money staying, or moving inside the house will save you interest at the 4.2% rate. Money staying, or moving outside the house will cost you 4.2%. If it remains outside the house, or is relocated outside the house, you have a choice of investment debt, or investment assets in which you can relocate that money to earn a higher return.

Investment debt such as car loans, credit card balances, and installment loans is not tax-preferred. The interest rate you pay is the actual EPR™. A credit card debt with a nominal interest rate of 11% also has an EPR™ of 11%. Repaying that debt provides a guaranteed savings of 11%.

A conservative approach to your Amount would be to locate money outside the house only if the EPR™ of the mortgage loan is lower than the EPR™ of alternative investment debts you may have. If your EPR™ of money inside the house is 4.2%, and you have a credit card debt with an EPR™ of 11%, it makes sense to pay off the credit card. Instead of paying 11% interest, your after-tax interest expense would be only 4.2%. By moving debt from the credit card to the house, you could reduce the interest you pay from 11% to 4.2% with no additional risk.

The increased cash flow could be used to increase savings that help you avoid future consumer loans, breaking a cycle of debt. The numbers make sense, but you must not replace that credit card debt with new debt, or the compounding interest will work against you.

If you pay off investment debt, and doing so increases your cash flow, what should you do with the increased cash? First, retire any remaining debts that have a higher EPR™ than your cost of borrowing. Second, do either of the following, or a combination of both:

- *Continue repaying your mortgage loan as a way of moving more money inside the house to pay that balance to $0.*

- *Continue accumulating savings to help reduce future borrowing needs, as a strategy for eventually paying off the debt with other assets.*

The House that Jack Bought

Imagine that Jack Brown is buying a $200,000 house with $40,000 in savings. He needs to decide whether to locate the $40,000 inside the house as a down payment. An alternative would be to locate the $40,000 in an investment outside the house and borrow the entire $200,000. A third choice would be to locate part of the $40,000 inside the house and invest part of it outside the house.

Jack purchases the house with a 30–Year mortgage at a 6% interest rate, paying interest only. He is in a 30% tax bracket and has an EPR™ of 4.2% on money inside the house. Using the entire $40,000 as a down payment would be equivalent to investing $40,000 and putting it into a safe, tax-free investment guaranteed to earn 4.2%.

Let's assume that Jack is earning 6% on an after tax basis on money invested outside the house.

Let's also say that Jack has $8,000 in credit card debt at 11% and a $12,000 automobile loan at 6%. Therefore, he has $20,000 in consumer debt with a higher EPR™ than his mortgage EPR™.

If Jack were to reduce his $40,000 down payment to $20,000, he could use the remaining $20,000 to repay his consumer debt. The smaller down payment would increase his monthly payment by an after-tax amount of $70 ($20,000 X 4.2% / 12).

Let's compare the $70 monthly mortgage payment increase to the interest that Jack had been paying for his $20,000 in consumer debt. With the consumer debt, Jack had been paying $250 per month in principal and interest on the car and $150 in principal and interest on the credit card, for a total of $400. Instead of paying $400 per month, his after-tax cost is now only the $70 per month mortgage interest expense.

Jack has increased cash flow of $330 per month. Assuming he resists the temptation to spend this money, he could use the $330 per month to accelerate the repayment of his mortgage (debt repayment). Or, he could invest it outside the house to increase savings that make him less dependent on future high interest rate borrowing.

Repaying higher interest rate debts to increase cash flow is typically considered a conservative decision. Jack could also take what many would see as a more aggressive approach.

Imagine that after paying off his $20,000 in credit card and automobile debt, Jack had chosen to leave the remaining $20,000 in an investment account and borrow the entire $200,000 to purchase his house. As long as Jack's investment was earning more than 4.2% after taxes, he'd be better off keeping the money outside the house as his savings would grow faster than his mortgage debt.

The Decision That Don Made

What if Don had no other liabilities when purchasing the $200,000 house with his savings of $40,000? He would face the cash flow / cash out dilemma that many people confront. Should he use the $40,000 for a down payment or put it into an investment account?

If Jack chose to invest the $40,000 outside the house, then his house payment, minus the tax deduction, would be $180 per month higher. Therefore, $180 per month is the net cost of investing the $40,000 outside the house. We know that Jack's EPR™ on wealth inside the house is 4.2%, and he can earn 6% EPR™ on his wealth outside the house. Could Jack increase his wealth by leaving the $40,000 outside his house, or is he better off locating the $40,000 inside the house and contributing an extra $158 per month to his investments?

Investment Approach*	Balance in 30 Years
$180 month	$181,315
$40,000 lump sum invested now	$241,949
*assumes 6.00% net after tax rate of return	

A large initial investment compounded over time can outperform smaller monthly investments adding up to the same amount. It could also be easier for a borrower to decide all at once to keep wealth outside the house by making a lump sum investment, rather than deciding each month to continue making smaller monthly contributions to a savings account.

The Mortgage as a Financial Tool

If your Availability is high enough to allow you to consolidate all debt under a primary house mortgage, that is what I typically recommend. A mortgage loan will usually have a lower after-tax rate than other types of loans. Any pay-down of higher external EPR™ debt using lower internal EPR™ debt will create cash-flow savings. To achieve a long-term goal of reducing your overall cost of borrowing, however, you must maintain your savings and not spend the money. I recommend setting up an automatic monthly debit to handle ongoing cash flow savings, or depositing a lump sum to establish a diversified savings plan.

Let's Look at a Practical Example of the First Four Steps

Imagine that you sold a house and received $60,000 after paying off the mortgage. Also imagine that you are buying a new house for $200,000 and expect to live in the house for 7 to 10 years. One option would be to make a $60,000 down payment and borrow $140,000. The bank would typically default to a 30-year fixed loan and accept your $60,000 down payment. Let's imagine you also have $20,000 of existing auto and credit card debts in place.

Steps 1 through 4 might inspire you to take a different approach, such as the following:

- *Based on Step 1 – Product: Opt for a 10-Year intermediate ARM. This provides a 10-Year fixed term at a 1% lower rate than a 30-year fixed, while still protecting you for the 7 to 10 years you expect to live in the house.*
- *Based on Step 2 – Payment: Choose an interest-only payment option to increase your tax benefits and provide a lower required monthly payment.*

- *Based on Step 3 – Availability: The lender offers to lend you 80% of the purchase price, or $160,000 as your Availability, leaving you $20,000 of opportunity.*
- *From Step 4 – Amount: Decide to borrow the full $160,000. Instead of putting your $60,000 into a down payment, use $20,000 to repay your higher-interest consumer debts.*
- *Paying off the $20,000 in auto and credit card debts frees up $400 per month in cash flow, with the additional savings from the lower interest rate and increase tax savings you apply all the extra cash flow toward your new mortgage, and find you'll be completely debt free on your new house in just 16.8 years.*

Even if you only live in the house for 7 to 10 more years, by the time you move you'll have significantly more equity in the house to reduce further borrowing needs in the future. This is quite different from the traditional path, but over time, it can dramatically increase your wealth.

Amount Work Table

There are two tables available, one for a Purchase and one for a Refinance. If you are buying a new house, use the Purchase table on the following page. Enter in (a) your total savings and cash available for this transaction, omit qualified retirement plans or money that is not accessible at this time. Then enter in (b) your purchase price for a new house. Enter in (c) the loan Availability you estimated from Step 3 (or know) based on conversations with a lender. Subtract the purchase price (b) from the Availability in (c) to determine the down payment you need as (d). Then subtract from your total savings and cash available (a) the down payment required (d) to see if you have a shortfall or surplus.

If you have a shortfall, you will need additional savings to buy this house. Consider buying a smaller house, or working on your Borrower Strength to increase your Availability.

Otherwise, enter in (f) the total of all your other liabilities that you know are at a higher net after tax cost of borrowing than the anticipated new mortgage. Subtract from your surplus in (e) the other liabilities in (f) to determine (g) your remaining savings and cash at the time of purchase. If (g) is negative you may be able to pay off a portion of those liabilities to reduce your overall cost of borrowing. If (g) is positive, this is the available savings and cash that you have that can be located at your discretion inside the house, or outside the house.

Determining Purchase Amount			
(a)	Total Savings / Cash*		$______.
(b)	House Purchase Price		$______.
(c)	Loan Availability**: (from Step 3)		$______.
(d)	Down Payment Required	**(b) - (c)**	$______.
(e)	(shortfall) / surplus	**(a) - (d)**	$______.
If (e) is <=$0 (shortfall) [STOP]			
(f)	Other Liabilities***:		$______.
If (f) is <=$0 [STOP]			
(g)	Remaining Savings / Cash	**(e) - (f)**	$______.

**Don't include 401(k) or other non-liquid investments*
***Should not exceed the purchase price*
****Omit liabilities with EPR™ lower than mortgage EPR™*

If you are Conservative, and the EPR™ of money inside your house is higher than the EPR™ of money outside your house, then you should consider placing all or a part of the remaining savings and cash toward the down payment to further reduce your interest cost on principal. If you are more Moderate in your approach, consider using any remaining savings or cash for investments that at least keep pace with your cost of interest, providing you greater diversification and increased liquidity. If you are more

Aggressive in your approach, borrow the maximum you can and invest in higher return opportunities to build additional wealth over time.

Determining Refinance Amount			
(a)	Total Savings / Cash*		$_______.
(b)	House Value		$_______.
(c)	Mortgage Balance**		$_______.
(d)	House Wealth	**(b) - (c)**	$_______.
(e)	Loan Availability***: (from Step 3)		$_______.
(f)	(shortfall) / surplus	**(e) - (c)**	$_______.
If (f) is <=$0 (shortfall) [STOP]			
(g)	Other Liabilities****:		$_______.
If (g) is <=$0 [STOP]			
(h)	Remaining House Wealth	**(f) - (g)**	$_______.

**Don't include 401(k) or other non-liquid investments*
***Include all mortgages associated with this house value*
****Should not exceed the house value*
*****Omit liabilities with EPR™ lower than mortgage EPR™*

If you are refinancing a house, use the Refinance table on this page. Enter in (a) your total savings and cash in other investments, omit qualified retirement plans or money that is not accessible at this time. Then enter in (b) your current house value. Enter in (c) the current mortgage balance on the house today. Subtract the house value (b) from the mortgage balance in (c) to determine the current house wealth (d). Enter your Availability you estimated from Step 3 (or know) based on conversations with a lender in (e). Then subtract Loan Availability (e) from your mortgage balance (c) to see if you have a (shortfall) or surplus of wealth in the house (f).

If you have a (shortfall), you may have no wealth in your house, or wealth that is inaccessible at this time. Consider what you can do to increase your Borrower Strength to be able to have more accessibility in the future.

Otherwise, enter in (g) the total of all your liabilities that you know are at a higher net after tax cost of borrowing (EPR™) than the anticipated new mortgage. Subtract from your surplus in (f) from the other liabilities in (g) to determine (h) your remaining house wealth after paying off all other liabilities. If (h) is negative (shortfall) you may be able to pay off a portion of those liabilities to reduce your overall cost of borrowing. If (h) is positive, you have house wealth that could be relocated outside the house.

If you are Conservative, and the EPR™ of money inside your house is higher than the EPR™ of money outside your house, then you should leave current house equity inside the house, and consider additional savings that could be used to reduce that interest expense. If you are more Moderate in your approach, pay off all higher EPR™ debts, using the mortgage as your only source of borrowing. Use the cash flow savings to increase your total current Savings / Cash in (a). If you are more Aggressive in your approach, consolidate all debt as mortgage debt, and consider relocating the appropriate remaining wealth (h) with any cash flow to higher EPR™ investments that provide additional liquidity and return opportunities.

Any cash flow that comes from the pay off of liabilities should be used to increase savings, or to prepay the remaining debt. To help choose among the huge array of investment products available for savings, I recommend you meet with a financial advisor before deciding your final Amount. Your use of cash flow should support your financial savings goals with enough safety to let you sleep well at night. When comparing various products ("buckets") for carrying your cash, make sure to consider the net expenses associated with the investment, as they will reduce your net Return. If you can't earn a return higher than your cost of borrowing, you may need to use your cash flow to repay your mortgage.

The completion of these 4 steps should move you closer to a resolution of your current borrowing needs, if any. It is a process that you can continue to use in the future to help clarify any borrowing decisions whenever they arise.

Step 5

Management

"Management" refers to your ongoing strategy for staying the course. The effective management of both your liabilities and your assets is imperative. You need to determine who will do the managing, as well as when, where, and how. Are you self aware, self motivated, and self directed?

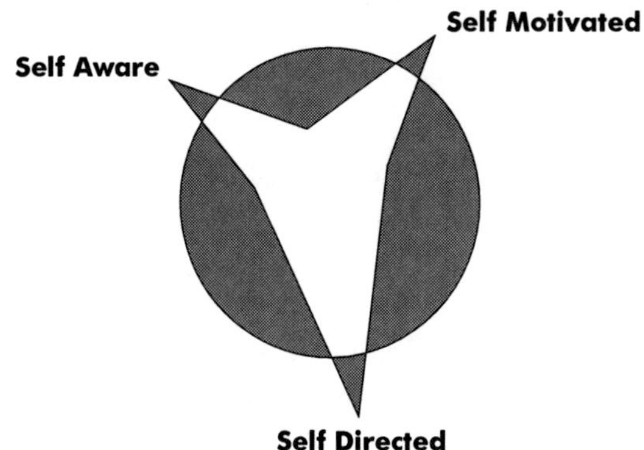

Are You Self-Aware?

You may be comfortable handling the 7–Steps in this book on your own, or you may want some professional guidance. How self-aware are you about your current ability to see this through in a meaningful way? Are you beginning to think about managing your borrowing to increase your savings over time.

The degree to which you are self-aware can be incredibly valuable in deciding how to manage your financial matters. If you find it hard not to spend your savings, you might ask someone else to help manage your spending habits. Or, you might commit to making automatic contributions to a savings or investment account each month.

As your self-awareness grows, so will your confidence. You may start to think differently about your next house purchase or the possibility of refinancing. Your new thought process will help you find additional ways to save; you'll consider how your approach to borrowing affects your ability to build wealth.

Self-awareness for many people means deciding to surround yourself with professionals to help you reach your financial goals. Explaining your personal goals and dreams to appropriate financial professionals can help motivate you to stay the course. It can also help you to remain accountable to others for your financial decisions.

Identify professionals who can help you in the following four areas:

1. Borrowing advice. Your lender can help you Borrow Smart Repay Smart™ by choosing the most appropriate loan for your needs. The lender can also provide ongoing updates to help fine-tune the management of your liabilities, such as when to refinance to lower rates.

2. Savings advice. A financial advisor can help with the overall management of your savings and investments to increase your chances of finding the right location, location, location of your cash flow savings.

3. Tax advice. A CPA or tax advisor can help you analyze the tax implications of your financial decisions. Taxes are a friction that greatly impact your ability to grow wealth.

4. House-specific advice. A Realtor can help you choose the house that meets your personal and financial needs, and determine what investments in the house longer term have the greatest return on your investment.

Having a support team in place can help to increase your financial confidence and clarify your intentions as you share your financial goals.

Your lender may help you find an appropriate financial advisor, Realtor, and tax advisor who will understand the concepts in this book. Or, you may have a financial advisor who also provides lending services and a team to support you. There are different ways to establish a financial team, but the end result is to increase your ability to make smart decisions each step of the way.

Are You Self-Motivated?

Many Americans now entering retirement have accomplished their goal of retiring without debt. By managing the right types of debt and investments, however, many could have substantially increased their net worth.

My hope is to inspire you to begin managing the wealth in your house. Through this process you can come to understand what choices are appropriate as your income and expenses rise or fall over time and various life events impact your finances.

Are You Self-Directed?

Would you rather pay off your house early or add $1 million or more to your retirement savings? When you face the cash flow / cash out dilemma discussed in Step 4, you might ask yourself, "Should I focus on cash flow or cash out?"

In other words, how do I borrow in such a way that I maximize the value of the wealth related to my house for; my self, my family, my heirs, my charities, etc. without taking unacceptable risk?

A conservative approach might be to use all the cash-flow savings found in the 7–Steps to help pay off your mortgage balance after repaying other debts, and then to begin to save. This would reduce the potential Safety and Liquidity of your money, but you would not face direct investment volatility.

A moderate approach might involve directing some of your cash-flow savings found in the 7–Steps toward the mortgage balance, and putting the remainder into an investment.

A more aggressive approach might involve all extra cash and cash flow to an investment account to help maximize the speed with which you build wealth. The trade-off is primarily the risk of investment volatility or loss, based on the product you choose.

Cash Flow - Prepay Now or Invest For Later?

Savings Found	Early Mortgage Payoff*	Savings Invested Over 30 Years**
$150 mo.	21.5 years	$150,677
$250 mo.	18.2 years	$251,129
$350 mo.	**15.2 years**	**$351,580**
$450 mo.	14.1 years	$452,032
$550 mo.	12.8 years	$552,483
$750 mo.	10.7 years	$753,386
$1,000 mo.	8.10 years	$1,004,515

**Assumes 30-year fixed amortizing mortgage of $160,000 at 6%*

***Assumes 30-year growth rate of 6% net after taxes*

In the above chart, assume that in Steps 1 through 4 you were able to find savings of $350 per month. You could apply that toward your mortgage payoff. In our simple example, $350 per month would facilitate a 30 year loan payoff in about 15.2 years. Or, you could determine that the $350 savings is an investment you can make each month over the course of a 30 year period, adding $351,580 in new wealth to your future savings. This is a decision I hope you have the opportunity to make. Ask yourself, emotionally which one is more exciting for you, an early payoff, or increased financial wealth?

Most of us have an emotional bias toward the simplicity of having no debt, even when it is financially advantageous to carry a loan. In planning when to pay off a mortgage, however, I encourage you to build in as much flexibility as possible. Instead of making it your first goal to be debt-free, consider setting a goal of having your liabilities fully support your long term goal of building your future assets based on your current, specific needs.

Increased Safety, Liquidity and Return could also be found through using cash flow or cash out to pay for your continuing education or a family member's education, even to expand your business. Any of those options might help you generate the highest possible return for yourself and your family. When in doubt, the direction that brings you the most peace of mind is often the best investment direction to take.

Reviewing the Steps

Review the 7–Step process any time that events change in your life or new borrowing opportunities arise. Events that may prompt you to revisit these Steps include:

- *Deciding to sell your house sooner than expected, or deciding to stay in the house for longer*
- *Deciding to remodel*
- *Change in marital status*

- *Birth of a new baby, or other addition to the family*
- *Change in income*
- *Change in tax status*
- *Inheritance*
- *New investment or business opportunity*
- *Change of employment or job location*
- *Major illness*
- *Change in the value of your house*
- *Change in interest rates*

When these or other life changes occur, you may choose to review the 7–Steps on your own, or with a member of your financial team.

One of the most obvious reasons for a review is to assess specific borrowing opportunities that arise when you purchase or refinance a house. Engage your financial team. Discuss how you can maximize your wealth on both sides of your balance sheet using these concepts. Identify savings that you can use to add to your long term financial goals. Look at this as a life long partnership where each party supports the others in their goal of building future wealth.

The Annual Review

Once you establish your financial team, you will want to identify a specific point person that will operate as your coach. If someone gave you this book, it is possible they seek to serve you in that capacity. When events trigger the need to review your current borrowing situation, those same events often create other demands on your time that make it easy to avoid going through this process. At a minimum, make sure that someone on your team will take the time to review your situation when needed, there is no greater commitment they can make.

Also, I recommend you plan an annual review with the point person on your team, using the 7–Steps as a way to identify any new opportunities. Set a date that will be easy to remember each year. For example, you might plan to meet on the anniversary date of your mortgage, or you might choose to meet just after April 15 each year when you have all your financial information together for your taxes.

If you are managing this process on your own, do an annual review each Thanksgiving to allow time to make any changes by the end of the year. For the same reason, late fall might also be a good time to meet if you are working with an advisor or lender.

I recommend a three-part review. First, note any personal changes that have occurred during the last year, to help fine-tune your current borrowing strategy. Have you undergone a career change or pending move that might change your Product need? Is there an income change, inheritance, or other event that would change your Payment need? Has there been an increase or decrease in house value that might impact your Availability based on any of the 4 C's? Do you have upcoming financial needs that could change the Amount you need to borrow? Have your liabilities changed?

In the second part of the annual review, look at market considerations. Have interest rates changed? Has your house value changed? Have the tax laws changed? Have new lending products become available? You might also reflect on whether your personal values have changed in ways that could affect your financial decisions.

The third step is to review cash flow in relation to your long-terms goals. If you had $350 per month in interest savings and chose to direct it toward paying off your mortgage, then look at the principal balance to confirm that you are on track for a payoff by your target date. If you chose to contribute $350 per month toward your investment savings, look at the balances in your investment account to confirm that you are on track to accumulate savings based on your future goals.

Management Work Table

Question 1									
On a scale of 1 to 10, how would you rate your comfort with Steps 1 through 5?									
Confused			(circle one)					Confident	
1	2	3	4	5	6	7	8	9	10

Question 2									
On a scale of 1 to 10 – how would you rate your self-motivation with your personal financial growth?									
Low			(circle one)					High	
1	2	3	4	5	6	7	8	9	10

Question 3									
On a scale of 1 to 10 – where would you direct cash flow savings now or in the future?									
Invest Savings			(circle one)					Prepay Mortgage	
1	2	3	4	5	6	7	8	9	10

Add the 3 numbers you circled in response to the above 3 questions. If the total is 20 or lower, I'd suggest you find an advisor or coach to assist you in creating a financial plan and building your team.

If you scored 20 or higher, you are a candidate to manage this process yourself.

Management Decision	
Who will I rely on to help implement my plan?	
My Self / Spouse	☐
My Team	☐

My Team Members:	**Name**	**Need to Identify**
Financial Advisor		☐
Residential Lender		☐
Residential Realtor		☐
CPA / Tax advisor		☐
Also consider: attorney, commercial realtor, commercial lender.		

Your financial team should have at least the four key responsibilities above. Your success is their success

Step 6

Protection

"Protection" refers to the approach you will take to always maximize the Safety and Liquidity of your wealth inside the house? Even after you have paid off your mortgage completely, the wealth in your house can remain within your use and control if you plan properly.

The Equity Line of Credit

Approximately 15% of house owners in the United States have an equity line of credit. The equity line of credit is one of the single most overlooked financial planning tools available today. It is similar to a second mortgage but offers a great deal more flexibility. You can establish a line of credit for at up to 90% of the value of the house, depending on your lender. The cost of doing this is minimal, it's often free, especially if you do it at the time of a purchase or refinance.

A line of credit can have check writing and even debit card capabilities. The interest rate is often tied to the prime rate, and you only pay for the amount that you use. Having an equity line of credit doesn't mean that you use your line of credit for anything in particular at this point, merely that it be established to provide maximum flexibility and control of your wealth.

The average American at retirement has about $14,000 in cash, money market and liquid bank deposits, according to the most recent Federal Survey of Consumer Finance. This money typically earns interest at a rate lower than the rate of inflation, losing buying power over time. That cash is an "emergency fund" for immediate liquidity if needed, and $14,000 won't go very far in a real emergency.

One idea worth considering, is to supplement the 'cash' emergency fund with an equity line of credit. Doing so might allow the cash to increase future buying power through investments that keep pace or exceed inflation. A 65 year old with $14,000 in a savings account, and no mortgage, might move the $14,000 to a tax free bond at 5% and secure a $100,000 equity line of credit. At age 85 they'd have over $38,000 if they hadn't needed that cash - while still 'feeling' safe with line of credit that was over seven times larger than their cash alone. The equity line can close simultaneously with your first mortgage, or as a separate transaction, For those qualified it could be set up through a reverse mortgage.

Aim for a credit line of the highest percentage of the value of the house, subject to any Availability limitations. Once you have an equity line of credit, changes in your Character (job), Capacity (income), Collateral (value), or Credit (scores) will typically not affect your ability to use the line of credit, even if you become ineligible for other types of financing. It's important to have the equity line put in place before you need it, as we discussed in our chapter on Availability.

Adjusting Your Line of Credit

If your house is appreciating, be sure to monitor the value during your annual financial reviews and make adjustments to the equity line of credit as needed. You can also increase the line of credit limit as you repay the principal in your mortgage.

In addition to Safety, this provides immediate use and control of the money in the house. Using an equity line of credit can help you borrow at the lowest possible rate in the event of a medical or family emergency, loss of job, disability, or divorce. You can also use it to pursue an investment opportunity. You might be better off selling investments for an immediate need, but having an equity line of credit increases your flexibility.

Consider this true story of a client named Tom: After retiring and paying off his mortgage, Tom continued to increase his equity line of credit as his house appreciated. His line of credit grew to $300,000. From 2003 to 2004, his stocks lost more than 20% of their value, but he used his equity line of credit to supplement lost dividend income and avoided selling those stocks at lower prices. When the market recovered in 2005, he repaid his line of credit without taking the loss from his stocks. When the market corrected again in 2007 the house value and his stocks went down in value, but Tom's equity line was still in place at a value that was much higher than the value of his house. He was able to use the equity line again for additional cash in 2008. This simple strategy has saved him tens of thousands of dollars.

Protecting Wealth when Selling a House

If you are planning to sell your house, you should plan in advance for access to any equity that might be needed for a future house. If you have a house worth $200,000 and a $100,000 mortgage, you have $100,000 of wealth inside your house. Let's say your Availability is 80% of the house's value, or $160,000. You would set up a line of credit for $60,000, allowing you to access that $60,000 at any time for any reason, just like cash - you only pay for it if you need it.

Before putting a house on the market, make sure you have established an equity line of credit for as much as possible. If the house doesn't sell and you buy another house and are forced to carry two mortgages, you can use the line of credit to support the shortfall. Another possibility is that you could sell the house with owner financing to expand your market, knowing that you've moved all your equity with you to your new house using your equity line of credit.

Realtors often claim that the less equity the seller has in the house, the higher the average resale value. This notion is based on the theory that the sellers are more likely to accept a lower price if they don't owe a great deal on the house. If the buyer offers $150,000 on a house that you are selling for $160,000, and you have a mortgage balance of $152,500, then you can earnestly respond that you need $152,500 to pay off the mortgage. Buyers understand and respond to this type of argument. They can identify with your concern.

Clients often express to me that they are concerned that their children would inherit a house with no mortgage, and not knowing the house's real value might sell it at a discount to simplify the complexity of work needed at the time of the estate settlement. Having an equity line in place allows a withdrawal to provide liquidity to the estate – liquidity that is normally unavailable after the death of the property owner. It sets a "high water mark" for repayment to "guide" the heirs in setting a sales price for the property should they undertake the process without the help of a Realtor.

Serious Money

An equity line of credit helps you protect the wealth that you locate in the house. Having an equity line of credit would allow you to use the increased house value to fund higher expenses associated with Appreciation, provide access to wealth if the house were to lose value through Depreciation, be threatened by Foreclosure, or for legal defense in a Lawsuit. Try to maintain an equity line of credit to the highest Availability for maximum flexibility. The only reason not to have a house equity line to your highest Availability would be a concern of Discipline Risk, that having money accessible would be too great a risk for spending something you would have otherwise not spent.

The following sections provide examples of how some of clients that have used this concept for greater wealth Protection. (The stories are accurate, the names have been changed.)

Protecting Wealth in the House	
Foreclosure	Use HELOC to bring mortgage current
Divorce	Use HELOC as shared expense pool during dispute
Disability	Use HELOC for medical and living expenses
Job Loss	Use HELOC for living expenses while job hunting
Depreciation	Use HELOC to make payments until market recovers
Lawsuit	Use HELOC to move funds to protected investment

Example 1: Foreclosure Because of Divorce

Stacy and Martin Carswell purchased a $310,000 house. The house is now worth $400,000. They purchased the house with an initial down payment of $50,000, and borrowed the remaining $260,000. Over 8 years of ownership, they have paid down $21,000 through principal repayment. Their wealth in the house is now $161,000 – the difference between the $400,000 current value, and the $239,000 current mortgage balance.

They are undergoing a bitter divorce, and Martin is living in an apartment. Martin can't pay his rent and living expenses while also paying the mortgage on the house where Stacy and the children still live, as well as child support. His payments to the lender have started arriving late. Both Stacy's and Martin's credit scores have fallen sharply. Emotions flare when Martin realizes he cannot buy another house with his low credit score. He refuses to make payments on the house, which Stacy wishes to retain. After two missed payments, foreclosure proceedings begin.

Meanwhile, Stacy hasn't found a job. She and the children move in with friends as they try to find a house to rent within the boundaries of their local school district. The house is sold at auction for $340,000, providing $100,000 to Stacy and Martin before related legal fees and late payment penalties. They both now have damaged credit, which raises potential interest rates for car loans, credit cards, and future mortgage loans. Stacy and the children move into a rental house. Martin is still renting an apartment.

Stacy and Martin lose any appreciation benefits that their former house provided. From the $315,000 they received for the house, they pay off the mortgage for $240,000, leaving $75,000. The money is split 50/50, leaving each of them with only $37,500.

They could have ended up with much more if they'd established an equity line of credit. With a line of credit in place, they could have agreed to utilize the line of credit to meet monthly mortgage payment shortfalls as they work through their situation. Payments to the lender would have stayed current. Their credit scores would have remained stable. Martin would have been able to buy a small house and secure financing with a down payment by using the equity line of credit for his down payment.

Stacy would have been able to continue to use the equity line to make ends meet during the transition. Using the equity line would have given her time to sell the house for closer to full value of $400,000, buy a smaller house, and retain her good credit. Instead of splitting $75,000, she could have retained more than $80,000 from the house by having the flexibility to hold on to the assets with greater liquidity.

Example 2: Foreclosure Because of Job Loss

Janet is a single mother with two children. After a divorce, she purchased a house by using most of her savings to make a $35,000 down payment. The house cost $175,000, so she borrowed $140,000.

After 3 years as an executive assistant with a large public company, she lost her job because of a merger. She was stuck looking for a new job along with hundreds of other candidates in the local area who had been displaced from the same company. Because of the number of qualified workers, Janet and the other candidates were forced to accept a lower salary.

With little savings outside the house, Janet missed two months of mortgage payments and found herself facing foreclosure. She began looking into lower-level jobs and found those job markets flooded as well. After six months of job-hunting, she lost the house through a foreclosure. The bank sold the house for her current mortgage balance, transferring her principal and appreciation to the new house buyer. She moved to a local apartment and began drawing unemployment benefits.

With an equity line of credit, things might have worked out much better for Janet. She might have learned that skilled workers were in short supply in another field of interest, such as nursing. Then, she could have used her line of credit to enroll in a two-year evening program at a local community college (paying tuition of about $4,400 per year), while working part time as a nurse's assistant during the day. Her line of credit could have covered tuition, books, after-school child care, and other cash flow needs during her nursing study. After graduating, she might have been able to earn more than she had in her earlier job as an executive assistant. At the same time, she might have discovered a rewarding new career.

In addition to covering tuition, the line of credit might have helped her maintain good credit, benefit from house appreciation, keep her children in their current school, and eventually refinance at a lower rate. The refinance might have allowed her to consolidate her equity line of credit into a new first mortgage before setting up a new equity line of credit with a $0 balance based on her increased house value. It's all about giving yourself as much flexibility as possible.

Example 3: Depreciation and Job Change

Eric owns a $200,000 house and has a $150,000 mortgage. Over a six-month period, rising interest rates and an oversupply of houses results in a dramatic 25% drop in house prices. The values of Eric's house drops to $150,000.

Meanwhile, Eric gets a job opportunity at a higher salary in another city, where there has been the same 25% drop in house prices. A Realtor advises Eric that to sell his house and move to the new city, he should offer his house at $140,000. After a 6% Realtor fee, Eric would receive $131,600. That would leave him $18,400 short of the amount he would need to buy a $150,000 house in the new city.

What if Eric had a line of credit? By establishing a line of credit on the original value of $200,000, Eric would have access to $30,000 to $40,000 even through his house value dropped to $150,000. He could draw $25,000 off the line of credit to put a down payment on a new house in the new city. Leaving the remainder on the line of credit as a buffer, he could rent out the first house for enough to cover current mortgage payments on the new house. That might allow him to wait for housing market values to recover before he sells the first house. Eventually, his new house might appreciate as well.

If Eric's mortgage payment on the first house had been $1,250 per month, he could make payments using the equity line of credit before having to dip into other savings or rely on his immediate cash flow. Thus, having access to the wealth in the house could give him maximum flexibility to avoid selling at a loss. In a worst case scenario, he would have to walk away from the house, but he would do so with his wealth extracted. He would still be able to buy the second house if he used the equity in the first house for his downpayment in the new house, and had a renter who would pay rent on the house he was keeping.

Example 4: Depreciation and Lawsuit

Five years ago, Martha and George bought a $115,000 house with a $5,000 down payment and a $110,000 interest-only mortgage. The house is now worth $150,000. Their wealth in the house is $40,000—the difference between the $150,000 current value and the $110,000 current mortgage balance.

George and his business partner each own 50% of a small flooring business. The partner dies in a tragic auto accident, and George becomes a 50/50 business owner with the partner's wife, Josephine. George and Josephine don't get along very well, but George needs to depend on Josephine, because each half of the business does 50% of the labor, installation, and management in their small company. Trucks, leases, equipment, and materials are all owned jointly in the company name. To continue the business, Josephine wants 50% of the profits since that is her sole source of income, but she is unable to help with the day-to-day activities of the business.

In an effort to keep the business alive, George offers Josephine $2,000 per month over 4 years to buy out her 50% of the company. She refuses and continues to demand her 50% share of the profits. Eventually, the stress of a lost partner and the drain on cash flow force George to shut down the business.

Meanwhile, reduced income from the loss of his partner makes George unable to meet his personal financial obligations. He starts missing mortgage payments, and other debts begin to mount. His legal costs to defend Josephine's lawsuit become unbearable. In addition to losing his business, he is forced to file bankruptcy and start over with a new flooring company.

During the two-year period when this takes place, interest rates are at an all-time low. Although George and Martha do not lose their house, they lose the opportunity to refinance and obtain much lower interest rates. The wealth in the house will be unavailable to Martha and George for many years, because the failed business and the lawsuit shattered George's credit rating.

If they had an equity line of credit, George and Martha would have had access a portion of that $40,000. After George's problems with Josephine made him shut down the business, George could have used the $40,000 to establish a new business. As an alternative, he could have offered Josephine a one-time settlement of $25,000 to buy out her 50% interest in the business as an alternative to receiving nothing thorugh the bankruptcy liquidation.

In this case, if Josephine had accepted the buyout offer, George would have been able to use his equity line to provide the $25,000. Because interest rates were favorable, he and Martha could have refinanced their first mortgage and ended up paying less for both mortgages than they had previously paid for the original mortgage. George could thereby have retained 100% of the business ownership, maintained his good credit, and lent his business another $15,000 to hire workers to replace the work previously done by his deceased partner.

Many Examples

Most people learn about liquidity at 70 miles per hour. These were real live events that were witnessed, but because of a lack of planning their solutions were limited. Life comes at you fast, and having financial options is almost always a function of planning for the unexpected.

Protection Work Table

Equity Line Needed		
(a)	What is the current value of the house you are now purchasing or now own?	$________.
(b)	What is the Amount you will borrow from your Step 4 calculation, or the Amount you have currently borrowed?	$________.
(c)	What is the net wealth inside your house? (a) - (b)	$________.
(d)	What % of the total wealth in the house do you want to have access to for either necessity or opportunity?	$________.
(e)	What Amount of Equity Line of Credit do you need? (c) X (d)	$________.

If you are buying or refinancing, set up the equity line of credit for Protection in the Amount shown in (e). Whether you are securing the equity line of credit with a new purchase or refinance, or as part of a separate transaction, consider the following questions:

- *What closing costs are associated with the equity line?*
  There are programs with most of the closing costs paid by the lender.
- *Is the rate tied to the Prime rate? If not, to what index is it tied?*
  High borrower strength can demand as low as prime - 1%. Prime is considered standard, with prime + for higher loan amounts, or other borrower strength or property issues.
- *How is the rate calculated?*
  Usually by adding or subtracting against the *Wall Street Journal* published prime rate.
- *What % of the house value will the lender allow for your credit line?*
  Ideally you want as close to 100% as possible, but if 80 - 90% is the best you can get, better to have and not need, than need and not have.
- *How many years will the line of credit be open for your use?*
  Most lenders offer access for 10 to 15 years, meaning you can draw down the money and pay it back as often as you like for 10 to 15 years. The longer the open period the better.
- *Within how many years must you pay it off?*
  After the initial open period of 10 to 15 years, the line is considered closed and no money can be withdrawn from that point forward. A new minimum monthly payment is calculated to make sure the loan is paid off over the next 10 to 15 years. The more years to pay off the greater flexibility you have.

- *Is the loan interest-only? If so, for how long?*
  Most equity lines of credit are interest only, for either the entire open use period, or less. It might be open for 15 years, but interest only for the first 10 years. For flexibility, you want the loan interest only for as long as possible.

- *Are you allowed to write checks against the line?*
  Purely a function of convenience, this feature is helpful if buying a car, or paying for college expenses where you can deduct directly from the line without having to move money first to your checking account.

- *Is a debit card provided?*
  Additional convenience consideration if you need more frequent transactions off the line, like if you are using the equity line of credit to provide financing for your business.

- *Does the line itself adjust automatically with the house value?*
  A new feature that allows the line of credit to grow as the house value increases, can work both ways in a depreciating market.

Step 7

Discipline

"Discipline" refers to your ability to stay the course. It is sometimes defined as "training expected to produce a specific pattern of behavior." Dictionary definitions include, "calm controlled behavior" and "conscious control over lifestyle." I like to think of Discipline as a state you achieve when you integrate what you know into your daily actions.

Since you have the Discipline to read this book, you probably have the Discipline to create a plan to put into action what you have learned. In doing so, you may form habits that help you approach borrowing as a way to increase savings for future wealth.

With a little Discipline, most people living in a healthy economic environment can create wealth over time. Many begin with no wealth, but through Discipline they establish a behavior of saving that creates substantial wealth. Among those who start with great wealth, Discipline helps to determine how well they can maintain that wealth and transfer it along to the next generation.

In Step 5 – Management, you learned that being self-aware, self-motivated, and self-directed are three essential building blocks for your ability to build wealth through managing assets and liabilities. The fourth building block is self-Discipline. Committing yourself to any financial Discipline is like joining a health club: it is an important first step, but the results also depend on having the Discipline to show up and work out. If buying a gym membership were enough, we'd all be in better shape. You need self-Discipline to stay the course.

In deciding how you will manage the wealth in your house, it is important to maintain self-Discipline in terms of how you borrow from yourself. Your house can be your sole source of borrowing, but if you borrow from yourself, you must play fair. Let's say you pay off $30,000 in auto and credit card debts through the refinance of your mortgage. Your cash flow increases by $600 per month. When you invest that money, you become the lender and earn interest from others. Remember, those who understand interest earn it; those who don't pay it.

Don't cheat yourself. You may need a new car in 5 years. You set up an account and save the $600 per month for 5 years, earning an average of 6% after tax. The account grows to $41,877. You now have the flexibility to borrow out of opportunity, not necessity. Will you buy a new car with your savings, or let the savings continue to grow and borrow because your rate of borrowing on the car is lower than 6%? If you pay cash, in a sense, you will be borrowing from yourself. If you use your investment account to buy the car, you can lend that money to yourself with interest and make the payments back to your investment account each month. If you have an opportunity to get 0% financing on the car, you might choose to borrow the money and subtract the car payment from the $600 you were putting into your investment account each month, allowing that money to grow while it pays for your new car.

The dynamic at work here is that you start to understand how your cash flow and interest create wealth for you, or for the lender, but someone is taking advantage of that wealth.

The Stages of Wealth

The stages of wealth development in the house follows the same pattern as your other savings. As you start a career, the first key step is to avoid a financial life event that sets you back financially in a way that it's very difficult to recover. These big financial mistakes are a result of not protecting what's most important, you! Step 1 - Protect what you have now from catastrophe. That means having car insurance, house insurance, disability insurance, health insurance, things that may seem like an unnecessary expense, but in reality they provide a moat around your financial castle to give you time to learn how the game is played.

Once you Protect yourself, Step 2 is to learn to Master cash flow. If you can't end the month with more money than you spend, the rest of the game is closed to you. You'll live in the debtors loop. Most of us borrow to buy things because we can't pay cash for them now. Our first experience of interest is how it works against us, and if you don't break that cycle you'll be the source of other people's retirement. If you Master your cash flow, and learn to spend less than you make each month, you'll have cash left over that isn't needed today. That cash can be invested in a way that earns interest. Each day that money goes to work whether you go to work or not. Its job is to earn more money. After you build a small cash cushion for emergencies, you can invest to earn higher interest returns.

As you build more cash, Step 3 become more important. In Step 3 - Understand - you learn about the products where our money can go to work earning more money. Mutual funds, stocks, bonds, ETFs, options - there is a world of opportunity waiting for your money. It's very important that you determine here if you'll take the time to Understand and invest yourself, or whether you'll seek a professional advisor to assist you. From my experience, it pays to profit from other's experience. Working with a financial professional now that already Understands the best way to put your money to work allows you to begin saving sooner. Why not learn from their mistakes as opposed to making your own. If you feel you can do a better job in the future, than a professional money manager, you can always make that decision in the future. An investment in eduation always pays the highest dividends - Understand as much as you can about the location that money can go to work for you, and you you'll be more engaged in watching how that money creates future wealth through compound interest. Your savings will earn interest, and the interest itself will earn interest.

Over time, your income and expenses are likely to increase and decrease. You will have money that you are saving and money you have saved. It's important to remember that wealth creation and management is more marathon, than sprint. If you become excited about saving, but you do so to the extent that life isn't fun now, you'll get out of Balance. If you decide to start saving later in life, you'll have to work very hard to catch up. Step 4 is the Balance of how much is enough? What's enough saving today and enough spending today so you stay the course?

Discipline Worksheet

Question 1			
What step in the wealth development process are you in today?			
1) Protect	**2) Master**	**3) Under-**	**4) Balance**

Question 2									
On a scale of 1 to 10, how would you rate the management of the wealth related to your house <u>prior</u> to reading his book?									
Poor			**(circle one)**					**Excellent**	
1	2	3	4	5	6	7	8	9	10

Question 3									
On a scale of 1 to 10, how would you rate your confidence in actively managing the wealth in your house after reading his book?									
Poor			**(circle one)**					**Excellent**	
1	2	3	4	5	6	7	8	9	10

You may also find that you operate in multiple stages at the same time. You may need new Protection after the birth of a new child, then a new job may increase income, but buying a new house stresses that income. That's where the Discipline and balance comes work together.

No matter what your current state of wealth development in Question 1, and no matter how well you have managed the wealth in your house thus far, there are more opportunities than obstacles. If your answer to Question 3 scores higher than your answer to Question 2, our time thus far has been well spent.

Continued movement in house values coupled with new types of borrowing choices will require a Discipline in handling house wealth during each of the 4 steps toward wealth development. Each stage has different needs that govern how you might utilize wealth in the house. A 65-Year-old entering retirement could easily end up living in a house for another 30 years, and a 30 year old buying their first house could well have 70 years. While wealth creation is important, most of us spend far more on our liabilities than we do in our saving. If we can Borrow Smart and Repay Smart we'll have more cash flow that can compound to create truly amazing personal and financial well being.

We've laid out a foundation for key concepts and ideas that set the stage for managing your liabilities in Part I of this book. In Part II we've provided a series of steps you can take to Borrow Smart. In Part III we'll provide a series of strategies you can use to Repay Smart. At the end of the day, if you Borrow Smart and Repay Smart you'll be able to minimize the cost of home ownership over your lifetime. This savings isn't trivial, it could easily represent $1M or more over the 50 to 70 years you'll live in a house as a renter or owner. That's money that you can spend now, or save to allow the interest to further increase your wealth. ▪▪

The 7-Step Borrow Smart Solution

Now that we've established the Foundations for Borrowing Smart, you can begin to take more informed action when you borrow. Even if you were not able to absorb all of the concepts in Part I, we've incorporated those concepts into simple exercises to build your Borrow Smart strategy.

While the Foundations discussed in Part I are essential building blocks for your perspective on how you'll borrow, the 7-Step Solution will help you assess the merits of specific actions you may take now based on what is appropriate for your current, specific situation.

Your Current and Specific Needs

Each person has unique current and specific needs based on age, experience, risk tolerance and other factors. The only real constant is change. Changes in one's personal or financial life often warrant changes in personal borrowing or investment strategy. Therefore, it's always important to consider your current, specific needs by reviewing these 7-Steps any time you experience a personal or financial change.

For example, imagine that you have recently financed your new house with a 7-Year ARM. Then, you learn that your company will be transferring you next year to a new office in another state. Reviewing the Borrow Smart steps again you realize you could refinance to a 1-Year ARM and save over $4,000 in the next 12 months. From a change in job location to the birth of a baby, any major life event could change borrowing strategies that impact your saving strategies. Over a 30 to 60-Year period, even small decisions can have a tremendous impact on your wealth creation if you take action to employ that savings to build new wealth.

Remember, good decisions, just like bad ones, compound over time. When in doubt - reach out to a mortgage professional you trust to identify any new opportunities.

Let's Play a Game

Imagine that you are playing a game with a goal of accumulating the most wealth possible based on your personal cash flow. In this game, you are given a variety of products that you can use to transport your cash; we'll call these products "buckets." You can choose which buckets to fill each month from your "faucet" of current cash flow.

Each bucket has different aspects of Safety, Liquidity, and Return that make them more efficient, or less efficient, in their role. This efficiency relates to the leaks associated with each bucket. Some buckets have more leaks than others and take longer to fill. Some leaks are really obvious, and some are only obvious over time.

Given that personal cash flow is relatively fixed for most of us, you have to decide whether to find and repair the current leaks or to continue to swap one bucket for the next, always hoping for a better bucket. You will come to quickly realize that the bucket you have today fills more quickly when the leaks are repaired, regardless of what kind of bucket you are filling.

Start Playing Now, Learn the Rules Later

The first time you played tic-tac-toe, did you win or lose? How about the second time? I'd guess that the first time someone showed you the game, you probably lost. I'd also bet that the second or third time you played, you were less likely to lose. Eventually, when both players understand the rules of tic-tac-toe, the winner is the one who can maintain their focus.

Like tic-tac-toe, the rules of managing wealth in the house are very much within your reach. Once you realize that you're playing a game, you'll be more likely to want to understand the rules. You can spend your entire life playing a game without realizing it. Or, you can learn the rules and choose to play with a higher degree of financial awareness. Remember those who understand interest, earn it. Those who don't, pay it.

CPSIA information can be obtained
at www.ICGtesting.com
Printed in the USA
FSOW02n1458010917
38151FS

9 781934 818503